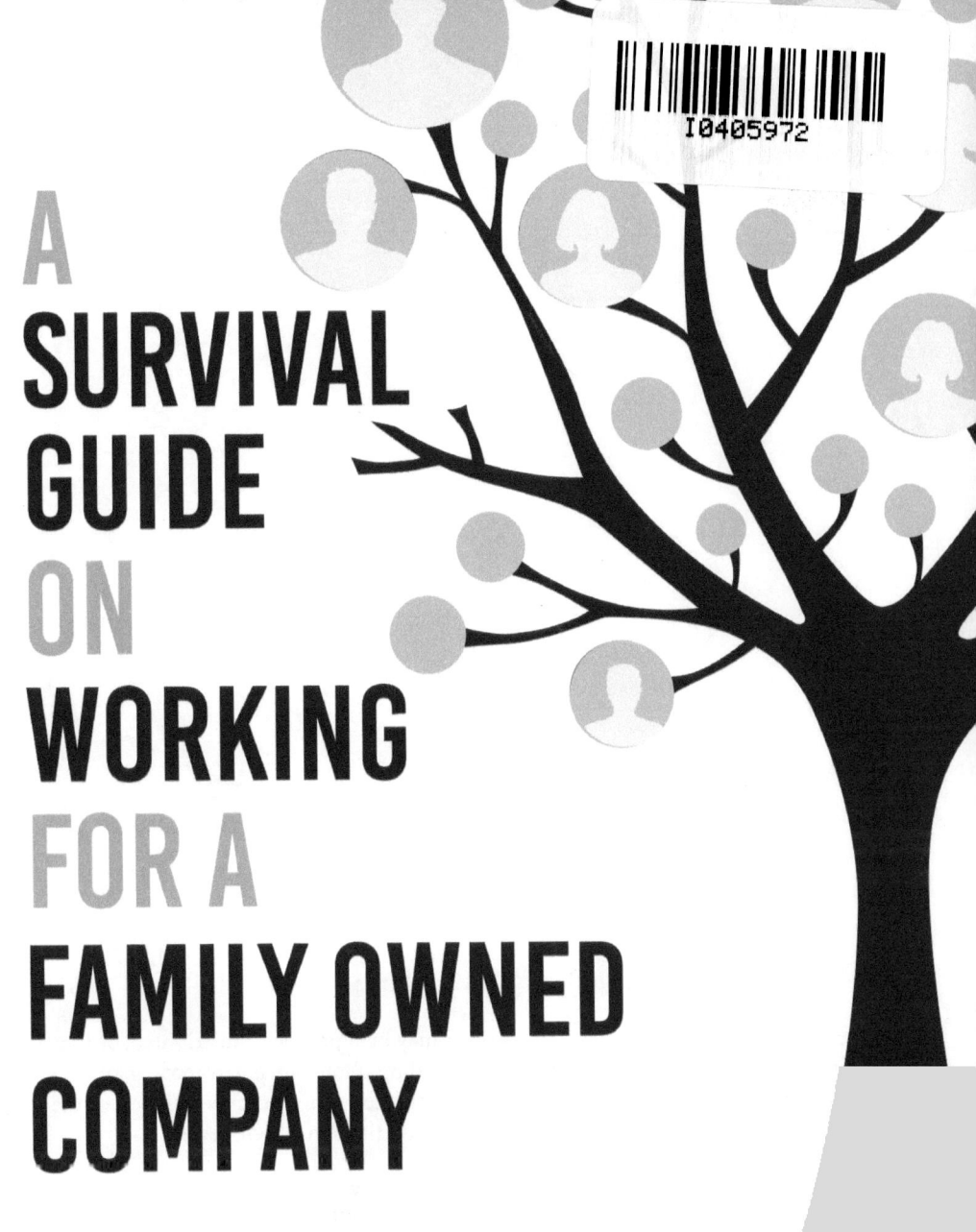

A SURVIVAL GUIDE ON WORKING FOR A FAMILY OWNED COMPANY

*What You **NEED** to Know BEFORE You Take the Job....and AFTER!*

James W Bender

Copyright © 2019 by James W. Bender.

All rights reserved. No part of this book may be reproduced, distributed, or transmitted in any form or by any means, including photocopying, recording, or other electronic or mechanical methods, without the prior written permission of the copyright owner, except for quotations in a book review.

Cover Design by 100Covers.com
Interior Design by FormattedBooks.com

Printed in the United States of America

James W. Bender

www.bottomlinesolutionsusa.com

ACKNOWLEDGEMENTS

The endeavor of writing this book has been met with a fair share of struggles on my part. I actually started writing two other books a few years ago, both works of fiction, and they both turned out to be dismal failures based on feedback from an editor that I had hired, along with my wonderful wife, Mary, who tried desperately to refrain from making too much fun of me for my somewhat pathetic attempts.

I decided to take a break from writing, but then along came my wife with yet another idea. Why you don't write about something that you actually know something about is beyond me, she offered with an endearing smile. Hmm, I thought to myself, maybe she's on to something there. She could be right. Of course it had to eventually be my idea, so I waited a few months before starting, and when I had finished the first chapter I finally told her my new plan. I had decided that I was going to write about something that I knew - the art of business and focusing on employees instead of management or leadership. What a novel idea! I had worked for many years in family owned or privately held enterprises, some smaller but many of them quite large. I realized that there were many nuances involved with privately owned companies, and that lots of people enter that particular employment arena with very little knowledge or insight into how to make the most of their time spent as an employee.

I owe my wife a great deal of thanks for finally steering me in the right direction. I want to thank her for putting up with me and coaching me along the way. She never gave up on my ability to get it done, and I could not have done it without her support.

I want to also thank my daughter, Izora, for suggesting a business book as my first foray into writing.

Last but not least I want to thank my great niece, Malaika, for providing me with my first set of writing tools as a Christmas gift several years ago. It was exactly what I needed to get started.

PREFACE

According to the Conway Center for Family Business, a research firm located in Columbus, Ohio, and the *Family Business Survey* compiled by consulting firm PwC, there are over 5,500,000 family owned and/or privately controlled businesses in the United States. These businesses employ 62% of the total workforce, and they contribute 57% of the nation's Gross Domestic Product. Family owned and privately held businesses are also responsible for creating 78% of all new jobs in our country.

By comparison large corporations employ about 38% of the workforce, but regardless of whether people are employed by or seeking jobs in family owned or large corporate businesses, every employee could use some additional insight into the intricacies and complications that occur while working in either domain. Companies can range in size from a small mom and pop store in rural America to Walmart or Amazon or General Motors. Employees need to know how they can best succeed while working at all types of companies, and this book is meant to serve as a primer for current and prospective employees. Everyone can use some additional insight on how to climb the ladder of success and navigate their future in whatever company they work for.

This book is meant to be informative, instructional and at times humorous. It is not meant to be an all-inclusive expose but more of a primer, an overview of a number of situations that all employees should be aware of as they seek or continue employment. As you read through the myriad of issues that can occur in a family owned company, and even a privately held company. I hope you will learn how to be on the lookout for various pitfalls, as well as for ways by which you as an employee can survive and prosper. Planning is essential to succeeding in business.

Finally, this book is an essential read for those high school graduates who have decided to seek immediate employment. Ditto for those college seniors who are about to seek post-graduation employment. Knowledge is power, and reading this book will arm the reader with the tools they need to find success and happiness in the workplace of their choice.

CONTENTS

ACKNOWLEDGEMENTS ... III
PREFACE ... V

Chapter One
Surviving the Interview Process ... 1
    Bring Your "A Game" ... 4
    Know Your Stuff ... 6
    Know Their Stuff ... 9
    Know the Interviewer ... 11
    Know the Organization Chart ... 12
    Know What You Want ... 15
    Know How to Read the Signals ... 16
    Know the Value You Can Bring ... 18
    Ask for the Job ... 19

Chapter Two
Researching the External Reputation of the Company ... 22
    Turnover Problems ... 24
    Weak Leadership ... 26
    Nobody Has a Clue ... 28
    Growth Pattern Fueled by Price Reductions ... 30
    Where's the Beef? Is it all Just Marketing Hype? ... 33
    Compensation Structure Too High ... 35
    Compensation Structure Too Low ... 36
    Legal Problems ... 39
    Niche Oriented Business Model ... 40

Aging Equipment, Facilities and Staff	42
Dead End Advancement Potential	43

Chapter Three

Surviving the Internal Culture of the Company	45
Good Old Boys Club	47
Stagnation	48
Nepotism	49
Patronage	52
Shut Up and Work	54
Inviting and Engaging	57
Appreciation	58
Collaborative	59
Team Oriented	60
Survival of the Fittest	61
Pandering the Boss	61
Innovation Oriented and an Idea Factory	63
Secretive	65
Open Book Environment	66
Bureaucratic	68
Autocratic	70

Chapter Four

Determining the Sustainability of the Company	73
Growth History and Patterns	75
Profitability	77
Highly Leveraged	79
Acquisitions and Divestitures	80
Geographic Reach	82
Succession Plan	83
Sustainability Initiatives	85

Exploitation	86
Exploration and Innovation	88
Cross Functionality	89
Less Hierarchy	90
Technology Capability	93
Written Business Plan and Strategic Plan	95

Chapter Five
Surviving Your First Week on the Job	98
Timing is Everything	99
Listen and Learn	102
Ask Questions	104
Attitude Matters	105
Notice Everything	107
Dress for Success	109
Meet the Top Brass	111
Social Media is Not Your Friend	113
Your Cell Phone is Not Your Friend	114

Chapter Six
Surviving Your Peers (BEWARE)	115
The Manipulator	116
The Liar	118
The Kiss Ass	119
The Wolf in Sheep's Clothing	121
The Leech	123
The Boss's Kids	125
Those with Tenured Servitude	127
The Undermining Bullshit Artist	128
The Spy	129

Chapter Seven
Surviving Your Boss — 132
- The Narcissist — 134
- Win at All Costs — 136
- Win at Your Expense — 137
- The Harasser — 139
- The Secrets Keeper — 141
- Throwing You an Anchor — 142
- Too Much Feedback — 144
- Too Little Feedback — 146
- Forgetting to Include You — 147
- Setting You Up to Fail — 149
- The Promoter — 151
- When Your Boss is the Owner — 153
- When Your Boss is the Owner or Manager's Kid — 155

Chapter Eight
Surviving Business Meetings — 157
- Meeting Time — 159
- Know Your Stuff — 161
- Be Prepared for Surprises — 163
- Bringing Food — 165
- Don't Be a Critic — 168
- Don't Point Fingers — 170
- Be a Problem Solver — 172
- Be Wary of Getting Dragged into Controversial Topics — 173
- Figure Out the Knowledge Dynamics of the Attendees — 177
- Figure Out Owner / Employee Relationships — 179
- When to Volunteer for Projects — 182
- The Meeting is Over - Now What? — 184

Chapter Nine

Surviving Business Trips	186
Substantiate Expenses & Company Policy	188
Spending Their Money	190
Watch Out for the Party People	192
Eating and Drinking Habits	194
Going to Bed	196
All Eyes are Watching You	198
Timeliness	200
Remember That Everyone Has a Phone with a Camera	201

Chapter Ten

Surviving Your Promotion	203
One Step Closer to the Top	204
The Good News	207
The Bad News	208
Management is Different	210
Success is No Longer Singular	212
Figure out Who and What You Have Working For You	213
Details, Details, Details	215
Hitting the Targets	217
Visionary Thinking	219
Figure out What's Important to Others	222
Planning Your Next Move	224

CHAPTER ONE
SURVIVING THE INTERVIEW PROCESS

So you have an opportunity for an initial interview with a potential new employer. Is this company a publicly traded company or is it a privately held company or is it a family owned company? You will need to make this determination upfront in order to properly prepare yourself for the interview. Maybe this is your first job out of college or perhaps this is your first job out of high school. It could also be a job that could mean better compensation and benefits over your current job. Perhaps this is your very first interview or perhaps it's one of many that you have had over the years. Whatever reason or reasons got you to this moment; you should now be tasked with being *properly prepared* so that you don't end up with a "thanks but no thanks" reply from your interviewer, or worse yet any reply at all. The military has an adage that they like to use - the seven P's they call it - Proper Prior Planning Prevents Piss Poor Performance. *This should be your new personal motto to live by because it will serve you well not only in your interview, but throughout your entire working life.* Being prepared will give you an edge over other people being interviewed for the same job with the same company, and can also give you an edge over your interviewer. Your goal is to gain the upper hand by being *better prepared* than anyone else.

Before we get too far into the interview process itself, let's talk about one very important difference between a family owned company, a privately held company, and a publicly held company, meaning a company that is listed on one of the stock exchanges and whose stock is traded publicly. Publicly traded companies, and a lot of privately held companies, have a decision-making hierarchy that is very different than a family owned company. Publicly traded companies have a senior executive staff and also a Board of Directors who are elected. Decisions are normally not made autonomously, and executives and Board members can be fired and replaced. Family owned companies are generally led and managed by family members, whether it's the original owner or the owner's relatives and offspring. Their authority is more absolute in practice, so generally speaking every major decision and sometimes even the minor ones are made by the person at the top of the hierarchal ladder. Family members tend to side with one another in decision-making and disputes, so other employees are generally on the outside looking in, with very little to offer in consequential situations other than input. You may get some influence in your job as time goes on, but if you're the type of person who wants and needs to be an authoritative figure (someone making decisions and not just implementing decisions), then working for a family owned company may not be the best choice for you.

Your interview could also be with a privately held company. This is the type of company that is not publicly traded and nor is it owned by a family. It is most likely a company that was started by an individual or group of individuals, and the company ownership is now held by a group of individuals and/or a group of investors, like private equity groups. The investors want a return on their investment and they are likely to hire outside people to manage their enterprise. The management structure of a privately held company is much more like a publicly traded company than it is like a family owned company. It is more hierarchal in nature and formation, with multiple levels of management. Sometimes top management has an ownership stake in the company as part of their overall compensation package that is mean to incentivize growth and profitability.

Let's assume you've thought about the issues above and you've come to the conclusion you are willing to interview with a family owned company, regardless of size. Perhaps your interview is with a McDonald's franchisee or with Cargill (the largest family owned company in America). It could be with a local auto dealer or with a local hair salon or maybe even with Ford Motor Company which is still *controlled* (not entirely owned) by the Ford family via stock ownership. Your interview could be for an entry level job. Maybe you're interviewing for a mid-management job. It might be that you're interviewing for a senior executive job. Regardless of which company or type of job category or type of company you pursue, you need to *be prepared to win*. Winning is your goal at the interview, meaning you get a job offer, so let's take a brief look at how you can best help yourself.

Your interview might be with the actual owner of the company, the top decision maker. Or in a family owned company it might be with one of the owner's children who have managed to scratch and claw their way into a position of authority (okay, there's some sarcasm there, I admit it). Then again, your interview could be with an actual human resources professional because the company has grown to the point where having a professional staff is a significant necessity. Regardless of the position of the interviewer, keep in mind that others may be watching in or sitting in on the interview. More people might mean that you get more nervous. It also might mean that people view you as a formidable candidate and they are expressing their interest by enjoying a group interview. Bringing your "A Game" matters, even more so in a situation like this one, so *be prepared*.

JAMES W. BENDER

BRING YOUR "A GAME"

Your "A' game means you need to be at your very best when the interview takes place. This is no time to be shy or timid or coy or hesitant. This is your moment to shine as brightly at you can, because if you don't you probably won't have a second chance. There are no do-overs in the world of interviews. If you botch the first interview you're history. If you shine, you get a second interview. You either win or you lose. Bringing your "A Game" means *being prepared*, being mentally, emotionally and physically alert, and having done your homework on the company and their interview process. Your mom and dad aren't going to be there to hold your hand and give you clues and cues. Your teachers aren't going to be there, nor are your mentors, your coaches, your spouse or partner, or your friends. The entire interview process rests in your hands alone, so look at yourself in the mirror, saddle up and get ready to ride this interview into the annuls of all-time great interviews, because that's what an "A Game" means.

If you think that you need a pep talk - get a mirror and a megaphone. Maybe you need to practice interviewing - use that same mirror. It could be that you need to shave or get a new hairdo - see a salon stylist. Perhaps you need new clothes or at least to take them to the dry cleaner for a crisper look. It might be that you need new shoes or at least to polish them for once. Maybe you need to wash your car - maybe you need a different car. Do you need to check on directions and parking availability? You've no doubt heard of Google Maps right? If you need to check the bus or train schedule - they're posted online. You may need to *plan* for transit delays or inclement weather or accidents - watch the news and local weather reports in advance. It is entirely conceivable that you will need to foresee the unforeseen. Ah, now that's the tough one because there's nowhere to look for that kind of insight. It requires thinking about inevitabilities, because let's face it, sometimes shit just happens and mostly when you least expect it.

These are all things that could make or break the success of the interview, so be aware of them *ahead of time* and *make plans* accordingly. Don't get caught trying to explain to the interviewer why you were late, or why you didn't get a chance to shave because you got home late last night, or why your clothes look like they just came out of the hamper. This is your Super Bowl appearance, so practice makes perfect and being *better prepared* than anyone else pays great dividends. Don't go out drinking with your friends the night before because your bloodshot eyes, red face and lack of attentiveness will cut you to pieces without you even knowing it. If you want your "A Game" go to bed early and get a good night sleep. Don't eat any food the night before or at breakfast the day of your interview that might result in something smelly sneaking its way out to permeate the room. The interviewer's face will not show amusement. Nor do you want to suddenly inform the interviewer that you need to run, and I do mean run, to the restroom for a few minutes. It happens, believe me, but just don't let it happen to you. Make sure you use a restroom before you enter the interview arena.

Here's a suggestion that an old boss of mine gave me years ago when it came to interviews and/or meetings with high level people of power and influence. He said, and I quote, "if you can't dazzle them with brilliance then baffle them with bullshit". How's that for strategy! Basically he was telling me that if I didn't know all the right answers then I should at least expel the appropriate amount of bullshit necessary to convince people that I was, quite possibly, a Rhodes Scholar without having mentioned that fact on my resume. Wow, what a ridiculous suggestion. Allow me to tell you here that spewing bullshit has the effect that you might imagine - it stinks and people can smell it a mile away. If you don't know the answer to some question, admit to the interviewer that you don't know, but also say that you will research the issue and get back to them with an answer. Interviewers like honesty.

I've had people show up for interviews an hour late and then try to convince me that I was the one who had the time wrong. They were of course sure of it. I've had people fail to show up at all and then call back asking to reset the date and time. This is not an example of putting on your "A Game". I've also had people who showed up wearing sneakers or sandals or jeans or a t-shirt. I've had people show up doing their nails while we talked. I've seen people answering their phone or texting during the interview. I've had people ask me if they could go outside for a quick smoke to calm themselves down a bit. I've had people ask me if lunch was included with the interview because they forgot to eat breakfast. I've witnessed people show up with their pet dog. Now don't get me wrong here, I love dogs, but they're not part of the interview process. I'm interviewing you, not you and your dog. I'm not kidding here. Interviews are serious business and you need to show some respect for the process, for the professionalism of the event and for the interviewer. Bring your "A Game" if you want the job.

KNOW YOUR STUFF

The "stuff" I'm referencing here means that you need to be sure that you know what you're talking about when you get the chance to actually talk. Recall the baffle them with bullshit suggestion that was told to me years ago? That is not an example of knowing your stuff. That would be an example of bluffing your stuff. It's important to know who you are, what you are and what you want to be. If someone asks you what your ideal job is, you need to have an appropriate, well thought out response. Telling the interviewer that you really haven't thought about it very much will spell doom and gloom for your chances of success.

Now I will admit that it can be difficult for younger people to know exactly what they want to do when they finally grow up and as their career goes forward. But what you can think about and say is that you want to work in an environment where you can make meaningful contributions toward the success of your employer. You want a place to work where loyalty counts and where you can take on additional responsibility. It might sound like a camp response, but it's a lot better than saying you haven't thought about it. The bottom line here is that you need to reflect on your own capabilities, your own ambitions and your own values so that your answer comes across as sincere and well founded.

A question that gets asked a lot in interviews relates to your personal strengths and weaknesses. Everybody has some of both by the way, so making an attempt to tell the interviewer that your weaknesses are non-existent is another example of bullshit. Knowing your stuff means that you actually know who and what you are. Think hard about your strengths and your weaknesses. One of your strengths might be that you are a good listener. Another might be that you are an avid reader and an avid learner, always looking to better yourself. One of your weaknesses might be that you tend to be a perfectionist, and sometimes that can stall forward progress because you're always tweaking something to make sure it's perfect. In other words, you need to think of your weaknesses from the standpoint of how they can also be viewed as strengths. You just don't want them to come across as weaknesses. If you want to get other opinions of your pluses and minuses, that's okay too. Get them *ahead of time* to make sure you know who and what you are. Get those from your friends, your parents, your teachers, other employers and coaches. The key is to know your answers before the questions get asked. Practice your answers ahead of time.

An interviewer might ask you what you see yourself doing five years or ten years down the road. Telling them that you see yourself retiring early will not be a welcome response. Not having any answer at all will also not be the best response, so make sure you have an answer for that question, not just to have an answer by the way, but also to think hard about *planning* your career rather than having it evolve in some haphazard, ill thought-out fashion. If you don't plan for your own future I assure you that no one else will do it for you. Again, know your stuff. Think things through with an advisor or a trusted mentor. It doesn't have to be perfect, but you at least have to have your thinking cap on.

A very important point is to correctly analyze the fit. The fit means the correlation between the exact job specifications, qualifications and experience level versus your own personal credentials and experience. Make sure you know that you measure up *before* you even toss your hat in the ring. If you don't have the qualifications that an employer is looking for then don't waste their time or yours. Know your stuff!

Perhaps your interviewer will be the top boss. Make sure you know in advance. This boss might ask you about the biggest challenge you have ever overcome. Perhaps this boss will ask you to elaborate on your biggest mistake, why and how you made it, and what you learned about yourself in the process. Wow, you might be saying right now. I don't want to talk about my mistakes, especially the personal ones. Here's the good news - this boss doesn't want to hear about your personal mistakes (unless you've been convicted of a felony perhaps, in which case you better fess up on the details right away), only the ones that you made while being an employee. Of course if this is an interview for your first job, the only mistake you can talk about is that you didn't start your job hunt a lot earlier. Get my point here? Your answer needs to address a mistake in a way that comes across as being positive, a mistake that you have learned from and that you will never again repeat. Again, answering these types of questions means that you know your stuff. You will also need to know their stuff.

KNOW THEIR STUFF

Their "stuff" means the nuts and bolts of the company you are interviewing with and hoping for a job offer from. I had someone in an interview ask me one day what we do here. They had no clue what kind of business we were in! They had not done any homework or research on the company, our industry or on me - nothing, just what do you folks do here? That was an example of someone not knowing our stuff. So I inquired of this person at the time - how can you possibly be interested in working for our company if you don't even know what we do here? The answer was something along the lines of - well, I'm pretty sure companies are all alike for the most part. I think I can fit in just about anywhere. Yep, just about anywhere but here I suggested at the time.

So what kinds of stuff should you know *before you show up*? For starters know something about the specific company and also their industry. If you're interviewing for a job with a local McDonald's franchisee, I'm hoping you already know the business they are in. No, it's not serving burgers. It is delighting customers by providing quality food at a reasonable price in a timely fashion. Sound like a line of bullshit? Maybe it does to you, but in reality that is their business model. Are they in the fast food business? No - they are in the business of delivering quality meals to people who are short on time or short on resources. They are also entrepreneurs, because most of the McDonald's locations are owned by independent franchisees, not the corporate office. Make sure you know the circumstances of the location you are interviewing with *prior to showing up*. Also, most McDonald's are open twenty-four hours a day, so recognize that you may be asked to work odd hours, especially when you just start out. If that's not in your comfort zone, then find another opportunity.

Maybe your interview is with Ford Motor Company in one of their manufacturing plants. What should you know about their stuff? Obviously you know the business they are in and their industry. So what other stuff do you need to know? How about the union issue - is your job going to be union or not? Are you interested in shift work? What kind of tenure environment will there be at the plant? Is there room for you to move up to a supervisory position later? What does it take to get there? What kind of reputation does Ford have as an employer, and in particular the plant and plant manager involved? If you're a female, what kind of harassment history does the plant have on file? Are you prepared for that kind of environment? How often has Ford laid off workers because of a downturn in vehicle sales and which positions are most vulnerable to such an event? Remember, even though the Ford family controls the ownership and management reins of the company, the fact remains that publicly traded companies and family owned companies rise and fall for a variety of reasons that are beyond their control. Things like the financial market, terrorism, wars, political instability and natural disasters all play some role. Recalls are another large issue that prospective employees should be aware of. What happens to new employees when recalls occur? Again, knowing their stuff means getting involved with doing as much research as possible before you get to the interview. *Being better prepared* is the key to a successful interview because you are able to ask more intelligent and meaningful questions. Knowing the status of your interviewer is also an important part of your preparation.

KNOW THE INTERVIEWER

Gatekeeper, Decision-Maker or Influencer? A gatekeeper is someone in the hiring process whose primary role is to conduct initial interviews and weed out the dead wood. This person is looking for reasons to weed you out, because at the end of the day their objective might be to cut the number of applicants from twenty to ten or from ten to five. These are just examples of course. The gatekeeper is not a hiring decision-maker but they are in a position to fire you before you even get to a second interview or have a chance to get an actual job offer. You will have to know or figure out very quickly if this is the person you are talking to at the interview. How will you know? Sometimes you will know from the length of the interview because it will be short. You will know from the type of questions because they will be general and there will be a lack of details on the actual job itself. You will know because there will be a disinterest in detail and more interest in protocol. Perhaps you can ask about the interview process at the start, as this may provide a clue to the role of the interviewer.

The decision-maker will come across right away as the person in charge of hiring you, most likely because they will be your direct supervisor. You will know because they will tell you. If I'm conducting an interview I am going to tell the person that if they are hired they will report to me. I want them to know because maybe they won't get a warm and fuzzy feeling about working for me. If that's the case I want to know that, and I want them to know that, or at least ferret out that feeling right there at the interview. I don't want surprises down the road and neither do you if you're the one being interviewed. Working and succeeding with people is a two way street, and it doesn't always work the way it ideally should. If we sense that we wouldn't be a good fit together it's better for all parties that we know that upfront. You will be able to figure out who you're dealing with via one simple question - are you the person who can offer me the job and if so, would I be working for you? If the answer to the first part is no, then they are not the decisive voice.

The influencer is someone who can either be your advocate or your worst nightmare. They don't have the authority to hire you but they have enough of an influence in the decision-making process whereby your interactions with this person can make or break the success of your interview. An example might actually be where the owner or top executive of a company is conducting the interview because they want to feel invested in every new hire. You would report to some other party in the company, but they have determined over time that they have a certain knack or feel for what and who will make a great long term employee. If this is the case, you have an incredible opportunity to make an indelible impact on this owner or top executive of the company. Screwing up this interview will be the kiss of death. As an example, how will you know if the owner is the one conducting the interview? You will know by either doing your research *in advance* or by asking a direct question during the interview. Knowing is always better than wondering. As I mentioned previously, this is no time to be shy or bashful. This is your time to shine. Ask questions in order to figure out the details of the company organization chart. This chart can be vastly different for Ford Motor Company (publicly traded and family controlled) than it can be for a local automobile dealer (most are family owned).

KNOW THE ORGANIZATION CHART

The organization chart is a document or computerized pictorial displaying the hierarchal structure of job titles and people within an organization. Obviously it can be crazy large or very simple based on the size of the company. Why is it important to find and study this chart? If you find the chart you will be able to determine where and how your interviewer fits into the company hierarchy. This gives you a glimpse into how many people report to the interviewer, who that person's boss is, and the kind of decision making clout that comes with the interviewer's title. Knowing this information is a powerful tool for you to use during the interview. Knowledge and information beget power and influence. You can come across in the interview as someone who is more knowledgeable than other people who might be interviewing for the same job. You will look like someone who actually cares about details, which will provide you with a powerful edge when the time finally comes for the company to decide on the first choice for the position they're hiring for. Remember, that's what this is all about - winning the job - and being *better prepared* than the rest of the candidates will help put you in the driver's seat.

Where can you find this organization chart? Start by looking online at the company website. There may not be an actual chart but you can probably find a listing of their senior leadership. You might also be able to find a company annual report which will also provide details about the overall power structure of the organization. In a family owned company, this will give you enough to go on because let's face it, the company is being led and managed by mostly family members, especially at the top of the company. Try to figure out who holds the most power and influence in the company. It might be the senior family member, which might also be the actual founder of the company. Perhaps it's not the senior family member, but a relative who holds most of the power by virtue of being the Chief Financial Officer. That's the person who has all if not most of the financial accountability for the company. Money talks and bullshit walks, which is probably why most Fortune 500 corporations are run by finance oriented executives rather than by sales and marketing oriented executives. There's power in holding the purse and knowing how to best use it - remember that during your career.

As you *investigate* and study your findings you will also want to keep in mind which parts of the company, or business segments, create the most value. Perhaps you will find that one division or segment of the company is providing a large majority of the revenues and profits. If that's what you see, then you will want to make sure that you end up in that part of the company. Working for loss leaders - business segments that are doing poorly - is generally not a good place to be for new employees because if disaster strikes there is a high likelihood that employees in that segment are the ones that get the axe first. The only exception to this rule is if you happen to be someone with business turnaround experience, in which case you may very well want to be the person who rolls in to take the loss leader from a loser to the winners circle. Then you get to write your own ticket for the future.

You might also want to make a determination of which person in the organization chart would do you the most good by riding on their coat strings. There is generally one family member in a family owned company that is seen as the rising star or one person in a publicly traded or privately owned company who is seen by folks internally and externally as the next Chief Executive Officer. Maybe you can even ride the coat strings of the founder or the CEO. If you get a chance to work directly for this person you may find your career prospects much more promising. It's getting this person to both like you and respect your work that becomes your objective. When it comes time for this, you need to know what it is that you want out of this new job if you do get an offer.

KNOW WHAT YOU WANT

This means that you should know upfront, *prior to the interview*, what you ideally want to have happen. You should know if you really want this kind of job in this kind of company. If not don't waste people's time! You should know what your career aspirations are for the future and be *fully prepared* to expound your virtues to all who are willing to listen. You should know what kind of boss would best fit with your personality type and what kind of organization would best serve your own reasons for working.

A good boss can help make your new job incredibly wonderful. A jerk of a boss can make your new job an absolute nightmare. Really think about the type of personality traits you would most admire in a boss - kindness, honesty, willing to listen, great coach and teacher, polite, understanding - things like this. The type pf traits you don't want to see are these - angry, explosive temper, nit-picky, criticizer, blamer, harasser, judgmental - this kind of boss will make your life a living hell, so learn to pick them out quickly and then head in another direction. *Knowing* what kind of boss fits your own style gives you a much better chance of success. If you don't like what you see and hear, have the courage to get up and walk out of the interview; no sense wasting your time or theirs. Much like shoe shopping, if the fit doesn't feel right then find another pair of shoes. Never settle for something that doesn't work or fit or you.

Knowing what you want can also mean your own tolerance level. Let's say you're interviewing for an entry level job at a locally owned McDonald's franchise or at an auto assembly plant. You might be expected to work odd shifts. Maybe that's okay with you to start, but how long do you realistically think you can work the 11 p.m. to 7 a.m. shift? You want to ask the owner or manager that question directly. Sure you might get some higher pay grade or shift differential, but in the meantime what will those hours do to your personal life, especially if you've got kids or want kids. Know what is realistic for your own personal lifestyle before you take the time to interview for jobs that won't meet your expectations. *Know who you are.* Know your tolerance levels. Know your best qualities and traits. Know your weaknesses as well. Everybody has weak points so don't try to bullshit yourself into thinking that you are some perfectly well-oiled machine. Be honest with yourself first and foremost.

Many companies, even those that are family owned or controlled, have great career opportunities that may require or at least provide the option for relocation. Are you *prepared* to do that if the opportunity arises? Most people don't think about this one in advance, and then later when the opportunity does arise they end up fumbling the ball and their career by telling the owner or manager that they aren't interested in moving. Why not, someone will ask? Well, it could be that you have a large family and everyone lives near one another; family is important you will respond. It could also be that you are the type of individual that doesn't like change, or maybe situations like moving create stress in your life and you don't do well with stress. These answers are all okay by me, but I would advise you to *think through* the options and opportunities for the future well in advance of doing any interviewing. Know who you are and what you will and won't do from a career perspective. Also, know how to read the signals as you progress through an interview. You can garner a lot of insight by studying the interviewer's body language and tone. You especially want this if it's the owner or hiring boss doing the interview.

KNOW HOW TO READ THE SIGNALS

I'm talking about learning how to be patient during an interview and constantly observing the various clues that the interviewer will provide you with as to their thoughts about you and whether or not you might be the right choice for the job and for their company. How do you do this? Body signals include things like the interviewer looking directly at you or looking away, raising of the eyebrows that might mean the interviewer thinks you're full of hooey, leaning in toward you or leaning back away from you, folding of the arms, looking at their watch or the clock on the wall which means they can't wait for the interview to be over, looking down at their notes instead of at you, getting up and walking around, looking out the window and more. All of these signals mean something about the interviewer's perception of the interview in general and more so of you in particular. The bottom line here is that you can't do any of this unless you *pay close attention* to what's going on. Being an ignoramus is not an attribute you want to include in your resume as one of your finer qualities. Go into the interview with your full attention to finite *details* and the interviewer's surroundings. Do not daydream or gaze out the window. That will be the kiss of death for sure.

There are other kinds of signals that you will want to read. One example is the words that are spoken by the interviewer and the tone of those words. Try to ascertain the sincerity of the words that are spoken. If you sense some cynicism then you can assume that the interviewer probably doesn't believe something you said. If you sense the interviewer is being glib then you can assume something you said is irrelevant to whatever the topic was at the time. If you hear a snide remark about your resume you might assume there's a bit of disbelief in whatever bullshit you mistakenly included as factual. If the interviewer does all the talking and you do very little, this means that if you do get the job your employment will proceed much the same way, so beware. On the other hand, if the interviewer begins a steady diet of more and more in-depth questions, then you might assume there is some genuine interest in you as a candidate. Yet another signal might be the interviewer leaving the room and returning with another company employee to participate in the interview. This might mean the first interviewer was impressed by you to the point of asking for another opinion before you leave the building. This would generally be a good signal for you.

Learn to observe. Learn to interpret what you see, hear and sense. Learn the buying signals that lean in your favor. Learn the signals that mean things are going down the tubes and your chances for a job offer are infinitesimal. If things are going well you will now want to know the value that you can bring to the organization because knowing this will help you obtain the best offer possible.

KNOW THE VALUE YOU CAN BRING

Knowing your value and being unafraid to share that value with your interviewer can be one of your strongest advantages when it comes time for the job offer. If you are someone who takes pride in being on time all the time, talk about it. If you are someone who reads voraciously for the purpose of learning more, this is the time to let people know. If you graduated at or near the top of your class in high school or college, this is the time to address that achievement. If you were on an athletic team in high school or college, now is the time to let the interviewer know that you have a competitive spirit about you. If you have made a decision about your willingness to relocate for a promotion opportunity in the future, this is the time to make that known. If you enjoy working with people and you tend to be team oriented, by all means shout this out. You want your future employer to know that it's not all about you (even though you think it might be, this is indeed a time to betray your sense of total honesty).

Share your virtues with the interviewer, especially if it's the boss or company owner, and it will endear you to that person as someone who is not shy or intimidated, and someone who therefore they should want to hire. It will say volumes about you as an action oriented individual and someone with enough self-confidence to try new things; to take on new objectives and new opportunities. Owners and executives want future leaders and future leaders are brimming with self-confidence, so don't be afraid to use that to your advantage. *Knowing* your value brings incremental rewards and opportunities. Sharing that value with others - telling people face to face - is the vehicle you will use to gain those rewards and opportunities. No one will know your finer attributes if you don't tell them! This is your time to shine brightly, to take advantage of everything you've done so far. Your next step is to get the job offer!

ASK FOR THE JOB

I've had many people (far too many in fact), come in for the interview, take all their time and mine, going through the ropes of the process, and then, when the opportune time presents itself, they never actually ask for the job. My question for them and to you now is - why not? Do they really think that they're such a hot commodity that I and others like me are going to trip all over ourselves and convene a love fest to woo them incessantly? Please….get a grip!! I don't think I've ever hired anyone who didn't actually ask for the job in person, and I don't think you will do yourself any favors by sitting around after an interview waiting for the phone to ring. More than likely you will never hear from anyone again, or you may get a polite email with the typical blah-blah content that is nothing more than a polite take a hike. If you want the job you need to ask for the job - period!

I've seen various statistics that reveal the main difference between salespeople who are successful and salespeople who are not successful. The revelation is this - successful salespeople ask for the order before they leave the sales call. Unsuccessful salespeople do not ask for the order. They wait for the follow-up call from the customer that will usually never occur. Twenty percent of salespeople will sell and book eighty percent of the sales. Those twenty percent are the ones that ask for the order! That's what you have to do - ask for the job. Tell them you're interested in the job and the company. Tell them that this looks like the ideal fit for you and this is where you want to be and what you want to do. Again, ask for the job and tell them you can start as soon as they want you to. Be bold!

I know, I know, you're going to say that hey, that might work for salespeople, but I'm not interviewing for a job in sales. That's where you would be wrong. Everyone who is interviewing for a job is a salesperson. Every time you go on an interview you are doing your best to sell yourself to the company and the interviewer. We are all in the business of selling ourselves to the people who we interview with, the people we interact with at work, the people with whom we want to be friends, and the boss or owner of the company we work for. Get used to acting like a salesperson because that's what we all are, like it or not. Just make sure that when you act as a salesperson, do so with a complete sense of honesty and integrity. Some salespeople are less than forthright and some utilize unscrupulous methods to get the deal sold. That is not what you want to do. When you ask for the job, ask with a sense of humility. Tell people that it would be an honor for you to receive an offer and to have the privilege of working for the company leadership or owner.

Now let's suppose you've gone through all the interviewing and you've come to the conclusion that you actually don't want the job. You don't need to ask for the job because you would just turn it down anyway. While every interview is a learning experience, it is also important that you do not waste people's time. If you've gone through the entire process and for whatever reason have come to the conclusion that this job or company is not the right fit, then do the interviewer the courtesy of telling them the truth, and move on to another opportunity.

Two of the things that you may want to investigate before you even think about applying for a job with a given company are the external reputation of the company and the internal culture of the company. But these things may not be readily or easily available prior to your interest in, and interview with, the company. So once you join a company you will want to take the time to thoroughly investigate both of these issue, because what you discover may very well determine whether or not you decide to remain with the company and whether you can succeed with the company.

CHAPTER TWO
RESEARCHING THE EXTERNAL REPUTATION OF THE COMPANY

It might be that you're just starting your new job for a new company. Or, maybe you're about to interview for your very first job. It could be that you've been at your employer's company for quite some time. Regardless of your circumstance, you need to *be very aware* of how others in the outside world of business view this company's reputation. Former employees have an opinion of the company. Current employees also have an opinion, but they are unlikely to share their true feelings while they're still employed with the company. Competitors of the company also have opinions about your employer. Bankers have opinions, venture capital firms and private equity firms also have opinions, especially if they're invested in the company financially. If your company is publicly traded, like Walmart or Ford as examples, then traders and analysts also have opinions about your company. Glassdoor is an employment website that is a great place to take a look at how past and present employees rate their employer in a variety of areas. Are all of these opinions important to you? Should they be important to you? The answer is yes to both questions, because *the more you know* about how others perceive your employer or employer-to-be, the better your chances are for choosing the right employer and for succeeding with that right employer. Pick the right company with the right fit for you and you're likely to be a happy camper with great chances for future happiness and success. Pick the wrong company with the wrong fit for you and you're on the road to misery squared.

Remember the seven "P's" from chapter one? Here's a reminder - *Proper Prior Planning Prevents Piss Poor Performance.* Part of the prior planning part means that you become a research and analysis sponge. You seek to obtain and retain all kinds of information about the company, including how outsiders perceive the overall reputation of the company. These perceptions, some of which may undoubtedly be tainted to some degree based on individual circumstances, will serve to be a barometer of the company's past relationships and performance with employees, competitors, suppliers, investors and customers. The past does not necessarily dictate the future, but it is an important indicator that you should be aware of and take heed to for your own personal benefit.

As I mentioned previously, knowledge is power, but obtaining that knowledge first takes the recognition on your part that you need to have it, and then the wherewithal to go out and find it. No one is going to do this job for you. You are the captain of your own ship. If you don't know squat about boating and you don't do some homework before your first voyage, you're very likely to find yourself in a shit storm out in the middle of a lake or an ocean without a single clue as to what to do next. Taking on water, finding out how long you can tread water, or fighting off sharks for your very survival should not be your ideal ideas of boating enjoyment. Using this as an example of doing your homework, you *should first* take a boating safety course. Then you should read your boating manual that comes with a boat when you rent or make a purchase. Then you ask an experienced boater to take you out for a trial run or two so you have someone with a functioning brain to make sure you survive your first voyage. This is called *proper prior planning*, and doing your research/homework to make sure you *prevent piss poor performance* on your adventure. The very same scenario holds true for making sure that you *do your homework* in terms of researching your company's reputation inside and outside their specific industry. One of the first things to look out for is a history of high turnover in the company.

TURNOVER PROBLEMS

Turnover, quite simply, is the historical occurrence of employees departing their company, regardless of reasons for the departure. This occurrence can be stated in real numbers or in ratios, and normally takes into consideration some element of a time frame. As an example, if company A has 100 employees and over the past one year period they had 15 employees leave, that would seem to indicate some degree of dissatisfaction within the ranks of employees. A 15% employee loss ratio over one year might be higher than an industry norm. Let's say company B meanwhile also has 100 employees and their employee loss ratio is only 3% over a one year period of time. That might mean that employees in that company are happier with their overall working environment. I say maybe, because that might not tell the entire story. Getting to the root of the story is your objective. Finding out the truth as to why people are leaving the company should be your real challenge. Sometimes it's not the number or ratio that matters the most, but more so the specific reasons behind those departures.

Examining the rationale for turnover numbers or ratios is important because it will enable you to pinpoint specifics if there is indeed an inherent problem. As an example, let's say that you're interviewing or working for a telemarketing company, that meaning a company that employs people to talk on the phone all day either soliciting business, or replying to customer inquiries (mainly complaints). I think it's safe to say that these types of companies have a much higher turnover ratio than other companies. Why? Most likely because the employees don't initially realize the stress levels that come with that kind of job. If you're soliciting business, there will be times when you get people on the phones that are very likely going to tell you to go stick it where the sun doesn't shine. If you're answering customer inquiries, you're most likely going to have a number of people that are very likely to tell you that your company sucks and that you personally are a waste of time and space. This kind of job will wear on you over time. That's why turnover will be so high with this type of company. In this case, it's not necessarily the specific company or boss that's the issue, but more so the industry. Know the industry reputation in addition to the company reputation, preferably *before* you interview for a job.

Your *research* may uncover a more recent pattern of turnover problems. If so, this is a time to investigate any recent changes in management or ownership of the company. Let's say you find that a year earlier there was a change in ownership or a leadership change at the top of one of the divisions or subsidiaries of the company, and during this time the turnover ratio rose significantly. This could mean that the new boss was cutting dead wood - people that were underperforming. It could also mean that the new person in charge decided to bring in all new people - people who have most likely worked for this person in the past; people that could be trusted to do what the new boss wanted them to do; people who wouldn't question change or challenge authority. This might mean that you should *rethink* your commitment to this type of environment, especially if you and the boss are not on the same page, or if the new boss is someone who doesn't mesh with your personality or personal work ethic.

There are lots of reasons for turnover problems, some to be wary of and some to put on the back burner. Recognizing if leadership issues are the problem is perhaps the most important step in determining your comfort level with both joining and remaining with any company.

WEAK LEADERSHIP

How do you recognize weak leadership? Weak leadership can best be described as executive level people who don't have a clue as to what they're doing. They don't have the experience, or the expertise to manage or lead others. They may in fact be the owner's or manager's offspring or other relatives who have been blessed with the right of passage and nothing more. *Beware* of this conundrum, because it is one that will leave you in the dust if you're not careful. I have had a number of bosses over time that fit this kind of description and they presented an array of problems for me. In many cases I found myself being the teacher rather than the student. In other words I knew a lot more about their job than they did, but my last name wasn't on the company letterhead. I found myself not only doing my job but doing their job as well, which made my life far more complicated than I wanted it to be. I was doing two jobs but only getting paid for one. I became the mentor and the coach, and it consumed way too much of my time and energy.

Weak leadership can also be defined as someone who either can't make decisions - someone who is, at best, wishy washy in their opinions - or someone who makes a lot of the wrong decisions. You can spot these people by looking at the performance of the company during their leadership tenure and by the amount of turnover in the company while they were at the helm. Strong leaders are confidant people who have no problem making tough decisions, with most of them being the right decisions. Weak leaders lean on other people for the answers because they don't actually have the required experience or capability to make the tough decisions. They require others to come up with the solutions and when the solutions fail, guess who they blame? Yep, that would be you if you're one of the chosen few who are tasked with working for one of these bosses. Strong leaders cultivate other leaders by leading by example. Weak leaders chase people away and cause turnover by virtue of being predictably uninspiring in their management philosophy and methodology. Which type of leader would you rather work for? Make sure as you examine the external reputation of the company that you are investigating the type of leadership they have in place today and in the past.

Many weak leaders also have a tendency to employ bullying tactics in order to exhibit and retain their self-imposed level of authoritarian rule over others. This is especially true in some family owned companies where the founder's offspring finally take the reins over. I have personally witnessed situations where the founder passed the leadership baton to offspring, but not the charisma, not the inspirational dynamics, not the foresight, and certainly not the level of knowledge or bedrock determination necessary to continue the historical success of the company. Working for a bully is not only tiring, but potentially dangerous. Bullies are predictably unpredictable in that you never know when or how the next blow up will occur, but you do know that it will occur at some point. Working in an environment where you are constantly sitting on pins and needles waiting for all hell to break loose is not a good place to be as an employee. If you ever find yourself in that situation, find a way to quickly exorcise yourself from that environment. Find somewhere else to work where your presence is valued, not persecuted. Ask questions of those who have worked at this company previously so that you won't be surprised by this kind of situation.

Many of the weak leadership issues in companies can be traced back to a lack of *proper managerial succession planning*, which in many cases then leads to the wrong person taking over the reins of a stallion without first being schooled on how to ride a pony. Working in an environment where people have no clue has consequences for the company and for the employees.

NOBODY HAS A CLUE

You're *thinking* about joining a new company and you're now *wondering* how you know if the leadership doesn't have a clue. You need to be a sponge and investigate by asking former and even current employees of the company. You need to determine if this is a company where you're willing to take a chance on betting your own success as an employee. Remember what I mentioned earlier, good leaders cultivate other good leaders. Poor leaders, who in reality aren't leaders at all, beget followers, ass kissers and snitches. Poor leaders rely on a combination of bullying tactics and surrounding themselves with lemmings that will follow them at any cost, many of them too ignorant to recognize the fragile reality of their situation.

Let's imagine for a minute that you start working at a local restaurant in an entry level position. What do you think your first job might be? Now I've never worked at a restaurant but I would imagine that if I did, my first job might very well be one that entailed cleaning the restrooms and the entire facility, including picking up trash in the parking lot, taking out garbage, unloading supplies from incoming delivery trucks and observing what others are doing in their respective jobs. Maybe my next job would be learning how to take orders at the counter or being a server to customers. Maybe next I would learn how to do the cooking. Maybe after that I would learn how to track and order supplies, and learn bookkeeping. In other words I would most likely *follow a path* whereby I learned every aspect of the business from the bottom up. Now imagine that I show up for work one day and there is a new manager, a manager that has never learned any of the day to day aspects of the business; someone who had never performed the tasks that I have, as outlined above. The employees of the restaurant, including me in this instance, are now taking direction from this newcomer who we are told is our new leader, but this person doesn't have a clue about anything. This newcomer has assumed a leadership position, but the owner or manager has never provided this person with any knowledge of the business; no managerial succession path that involved learning every aspect of what goes on in a restaurant. Who is at fault when things don't go well and begin to fall apart - the newcomer or the owner? I'm sure you can guess the correct answer here. It's the boss, but if you're one of the employees you really don't care who's at fault, you just care about the impact on you, your job and your future with the company. Let's say *you did some homework* and you found out about all of the above *before* you took the job. Would you still take the job?

Maybe worse than certain management not knowing anything at all, would be when a new manager takes over and makes the decision to spend almost no time at the company. He or she is thinking that they're golden, no chance of being fired, so why not just leave early a lot, take days off without telling anyone, show up at eleven in the morning, or take a two hour lunch from twelve to two, and then leave at three. This would be the epitome of ignorance, arrogance and selfishness. Think about how hard it would be to work for someone like that, unless of course you're one of the chosen few who have taken on the unenviable role of kissing their ass every day in order to survive. Believe me; I've known plenty of people who have done just that.

There are of course some new managers that do very well, but I have seen way too much of the other side of the coin. Most of these people who take over the reins of a company are endeared with some self-serving sense of entitlement, and that gives them an air of arrogance that is indeed hard to swallow for most people. Founders and owners would do their heir apparent a huge favor by forcing them to find external work for some period of time before entering the boss's work arena. In this way they will gain a true understanding of what it's like to be an employee, to take orders, to *accept authority*, and to work with others as peers instead of as the boss's chosen one. Just because the owner or founder or top executive does well with a company does not mean that anyone else will do well with the company. Owners and founders have a special bond with their company. No one else will ever have that same feeling or bond. It's impossible for that to occur because no one else put in the blood, sweat and tears that went along with building the company. Those of you looking to work in a company when the transfer of power takes place need to be very much aware of the changes that are likely to take place. Nothing works quite the same way after the owner or founder or lead executive steps aside for the next in line, and a lot of people on the outside see that happening every day. Know how to secure that information and recognize the potential for instability.

Another area to examine in a company is the reason for revenue growth. I'm sure you've all seen record revenue announcements made by companies in the past. When you hear that news, do you ever stop to think about the reasons for the surprise revenue growth results?

GROWTH PATTERN FUELED BY PRICE REDUCTIONS

Here is a simplistic example of what I mean by fueling growth via reducing prices. Let's say that you decide to have a lemonade stand on the corner near your house and have a two day sale over the weekend. You have gathered all the necessary supplies to both make and sell your product, which is lemonade. You have determined that your costs are going to be $.50 per glass based on an 8oz. plastic cup. In order to break even based on all the supplies you have already bought, you will need to sell 100 glasses of lemonade, meaning your gross sales need to be $50.00 just to break even. Any sales over 100 glasses of lemonade will result in pure profit. Your intention is to sell each glass for cost with the hope of selling 200 glasses of lemonade for a 100% profit margin.

Day one of your sale goes poorly, with sales of only 10 glasses of lemonade, generating $5.00 of revenue. Your palms get sweaty, you panic, and then you decide to reduce your price per glass to $.25 on day two, half your original price point, with the objective of selling enough lemonade to at least break even. Your sales on day two go through the roof compared to day one and you are beaming with excitement at your initial thoughts of success. You later realize that your big day resulted in a whopping 100 glasses of lemonade being sold. Your sales revenue for the day is $25.00, a big jump over day one sales of $5.00. Your smile is as wide as the Mississippi River and you can't wait to tell your friends. Unfortunately your total sales number for both days is below the price point that was necessary to break even. You needed $50.00 in sales to break even, and you only achieved a total of $30.00. You assumed that by reducing your price point you would increase your sales, which you in fact did, but you neglected to determine the number of glasses you would need to sell on day two at $.25 per glass to reach your breakeven point. While you are rejoicing your huge day two sales numbers, you have not yet realized that you lost $20.00 for the weekend. This is an example of how reducing your price point to increase sales numbers can mask the reality of the overall revenue and net margin numbers. Sure, your sales numbers increased by 1,000% from day two over day one, but you lost money in the end. This scenario can also happen to small, medium and large size companies, not just neighborhood lemonade stands.

The *devil is in the details*, which are not always visible externally, so you need to sometimes dig into the details to find out why your company has experienced their growth. Is it real or is it a façade being played, a numbers game that misrepresents the real reasons for the revenue growth.

I have seen this scenario play out in my career, where revenue numbers look surreal on paper, but in reality the company is losing money on every dollar of revenue because of a price reduction that is unsustainable for the future stability of the company. Would you want to join a company that only looked good on paper? I think that most of you would prefer to work for a company where revenues were generated at a profitable margin, which would ensure that the company will be able to maintain its employees and sustain growth in the future.

I have seen companies in the past that consistently tried to generate additional revenues by discounting their pricing to certain types of customers. Sometimes this process worked, but only for a very short period of time. Why is that you ask? Eventually competitors caught on to what was going on and guess what they did next? They started to discount their prices even lower, which then resulted in the entire industry following suit. How do you think that whole scenario worked out for everyone? Before long every company was doing the same discounting and everyone's revenue started to actually drop because of the discounting. What started out as a seemingly good idea ended up being a disaster for the entire industry. What's even worse is that every company continued with the discounting methodology because they were each afraid if they didn't do it, that they would lose market share to their competition. This was an example of a company making the wrong choices when it came time to increase revenues. This is the type of information that becomes known externally, and therefore it's the type of information you want to know and consider before you take a job with that company.

As it relates to the above example, you might also want to know something about how that organization promotes itself to their customer base. If they have to reduce themselves to discounting their services or products to make sales, then you would have to wonder about the substance of their sales pitch as well.

WHERE'S THE BEEF? IS IT ALL JUST MARKETING HYPE?

I once worked for someone who could charm the skin off a snake. What does that mean you ask? It means that the words, tone, appeal and delivery of the message were so powerful that this individual could sell ice to an Eskimo, fur coats to nudists and condoms to ninety year old men. The overall charm and wit of the message was filled with such mesmerizing magnetism that people didn't even stop to think about the actual quality of the product or service being sold, or even its practical usability. Translation - sometimes you need to be extremely careful not to get bowled over by a company's marketing-oriented delivery of a message. After all, the whole sales pitch may in fact be total bullshit; filled with exaggerated hyperbole, fictitious numbers, misstated facts, inaccurate quality initiatives and results, and proverbial smoke being blown up your ass. In addition, all of this can be performed for you by some sensually provocative voice or some highly attractive spokesperson, or maybe both.

Did you really think that all those ads you see on your televisions screen that provide you with sensual feelings of delight are done so with the intent of providing the real nuts and bolts of what the company is trying to sell? No, many of those ads are meant to divert you from the actual reality of the product or service being sold, and instead to reel you in to an aura of awe and wonderment, such that you feel compelled to buy from the company. Is it beef or is it bullshit? More often than not it's pure bullshit, so *pay attention* to finding the beef.

If you come across a company that has as its main claim to fame a series of amusing ads with captivating and attractive spokesmen of high notoriety, then you should be prepared to do some homework and really dig hard for the beef behind the beefcake. If you constantly see ads that feature sensually looking and sounding spokeswomen, you need to dig hard to find the beef behind the beauty.

All of us can be fooled into believing that a company and/or a company's product or service is better than it really is by virtue of what we see and by what we are being told to feel and think. That's what ads do - they are designed to herd us into a grouping; to put us where we will all fit together like pieces of a puzzle. We then become a customer type that can be further exploited by similar ads in the future that appeal to our historical pattern of sensory perspectives. This is marketing and advertising at its best, but it is not the beef. It is not the nuts and bolts of what a company does for its customers. You want the real deal not the raw deal, so be aware of how all of this hype can be designed to produce a company's external reputation. Your success will depend on the reality of a company's performance and not the advertising face or persona of the company.

Legend has it that a former owner of a company I once worked for used to brag about the company objective of only selling their services to every person in America just once. I would guess that this message rang hollow when it came time to produce customer quality and loyalty ratings. What do you suppose that message meant to the employees of that company? Once again legend has it that since the owner didn't care much about quality, that's exactly what the company served its customers.

What do you think that statement meant to customers once they heard this news? It meant that fewer and fewer customers were going to take the risk of using the services of this company, which then led to a financial downturn that eventually required the company to either find an unwitting buyer or file for bankruptcy protection. Sure, the message was one of honesty from the owner's perspective, but also one of incredibly poor judgment and visionary thinking; at the end of the day they were just a con artist. Would you want to work in that kind of environment?

A few other things you want to take a look at when you're first thinking about joining or even remaining with a company are their compensation structures. Is the company fair, or do they is their pay scale too high, or is it ridiculously low? You want to ferret out the details as soon as you can in order to figure out the internal compensation dynamics of the company.

COMPENSATION STRUCTURE TOO HIGH

Why would a company have a compensation structure that is looked at by many on the outside as far too high and far too generous? Maybe it's the only way they can recruit people to join the company. Maybe the reputation of the company is so bad that money is the only mechanism they have to land employees, or to keep employees. Maybe the company uses money as a ball and chain around the necks of their employees, knowing full well that once people are used to a certain standard of living they will be reluctant to leave that status.

So what do you do when you learn that the normal salary structure for the job you are applying for is $35,000 - $45,000 per year, and the company offers you $60,000 per year to start with a guaranteed end of year bonus on top? Do you tell them to bugger off? Do you tell them they're bloody crazy? Or do you smile, nod your head, hold out your hand to seal the deal, and say thank you, all the while knowing your days are numbered? Your days are probably numbered because these types of offers from these types of companies normally result in very high, in fact unreasonably high levels of expectation of productivity from their employees. Your boss and their bosses will be watching you very carefully, looking for any reason at all to either knock down that high salary of yours, or even worse yet to show you the exit door. Unreasonably high compensation means high levels of scrutiny and low levels of tolerance. Keep doing well and you get to stay. Screw up once and you're nothing but a fart in a windstorm, ushered out the door with surprising speed.

There is of course an exception to this rule of overzealous micromanagement, and that is if you are a real superstar of an employee. Join a company with higher than normal compensation pay scales and you are under the proverbial microscope from day one, but if you excel beyond your owner or manager's wildest dreams you may end up with the job of a lifetime, at least for a while that is. If you are the aggressive personality type, always willing to accept any challenge with gusto, then maybe a company with high wage scales might be right for you. It certainly is one way to move yourself up the standard of living chart, and maybe even impress your spouse, your parents, your neighbors, your friends, your financial advisor, even your dog because you can now afford more biscuits and a better doggie bed. If money is the only thing that matters to you then by all means go for this type of job. Just remember to be wary every day, and I do mean every day, of being bushwhacked without any notice.

There are also companies out there in the real world that have a reputation of paying their employees too little. Why would they do this you ask? Well, you're about to find out.

COMPENSATION STRUCTURE TOO LOW

Many companies simply do not have the wherewithal financially to pay their employees a lot. Take for instance a local Burger King franchise in a small town. The cost of owning this type of franchise is fairly high, and most likely the gross revenues of a small town restaurant is not anywhere near what it might be in midtown Manhattan or downtown Chicago. The owner will adjust the pay scale to fit the store revenue and predicted profit margin based on a conservative annual revenue target, because let's face it, there are no guarantees with this kind of business. Maybe the store hits its target and maybe it doesn't, and this is especially true if it's the first or second year of this particular franchise being in business. Maybe this Burger King can only afford to pay $8.00 per hour to its new employees, whereas in New York that wage might be $15.00 per hour. The point here is that many employers will set wage scales at a level where they believe they can both make a profit and recruit and retain good employees. Maybe this type of employer values loyalty and dedication more than they do being an overachiever. You just need to *examine* why employers decide to set compensation structures the way they do, and by doing so you will gain an in-depth *understanding* of their business model and their rationale for making the decisions that they do.

I once knew of an employer who knowingly and arbitrarily decided that the compensation structure of the company was going to be at the absolute low end of their particular industry. There was no way they were going to overpay someone and they didn't care who it was that they were talking to or about. They could have been interviewing Bill Gates for their top technology position with a strong leaning toward research and development, but they sure as hell weren't about to pay him any more than what their internal compensation chart told them to. That would be an example of being incredibly penny wise and pound foolish. This particular company manager never ever found a real superstar as an employee in any discipline because they were all chased away by virtue of a reputation for having an unreasonably low compensation structure. We all want to feel that we're being paid for our worth. If we feel that we're being taken advantage of, then we are not likely to work for that company.

There are many good reasons for a company to set their compensation structures at a lower scale than their competitors, although they at least want to be in a range that is reasonable and easily explained to others. They do not want to have a reputation in their industry as being the lowest paying employer because that will get them nowhere fast. Every company needs to keep an eye on their competition and know what the others are paying for various positions. It's perhaps even more important for some departments over others.

Let's take the sales department as an example. I think we can all agree that every company needs sales and if they are the type of company that garners sales by hiring salespeople, they then need to be able to hire the best salespeople in order to achieve their very best sales growth. You beat the competition by various methods - better pricing, better service, better products, better quality, better cost structure and better salespeople. In order to hire and retain the best salespeople you cannot have a compensation structure that is significantly lower than your competition. Let me rephrase that - you can have a lower pay structure, but that structure will eventually bite you in the ass and you will most likely never have the best salespeople. Salespeople are primarily motivated by two things - money and the desire to win. *Winning* means making the sale. The reward for winning is making more money. It really is that simple. Salespeople want to be paid well, much more so than a congratulatory letter or receiving some plaque that goes on the wall. It's important for a company that needs and wants salespeople to not have a reputation for having a low compensation structure.

Make sure you figure out if your company is on the low end of the compensation structure curve. If you like money and you like being paid for your worth, the low end company may not be your ideal choice. Yet one more issue to take into consideration is a company that has a history of legal problems.

LEGAL PROBLEMS

What kinds of legal problems are there? One very large legal problem could be a rumor mill suggesting near term bankruptcy proceedings. If you hear these rumors then you probably want to reconsider your employment situation. Working in this type of environment is taxing at best because you never know what the next day or hour will bring. Top executives, including the owner or founder of a company, will not be telling the truth to their employees. They will of course be expounding on a bright future that lies ahead for the company, and that the rumors are just that, unsubstantiated lies and accusations. They are pretty much forced into that situation by lenders and creditors who do not want the rumor mill to further damage an already dire financial situation, nor to further tarnish the company's reputation. Being employed in a potential or actual bankruptcy situation is not just lacking in any fun, but extremely stressful every single day that you show up for work.

Another legal situation that can spell trouble for a company revolves around consumer litigation. Let's say that your employer-to-be produces a product that turns out to be defective and this results in some kind of harmful effect on a large group of its customers. Several consumers band together and start a class action law suit against the company. The class action suit then picks up steam as more consumers become aware of the problem and before long the suit becomes a multimillion dollar fiasco with significant financial impact on the company's future ability to even survive. Maybe the company does survive but their reputation is so severely damaged that it results in a decline in revenues and profits for many years afterwards. You most likely would not want to end up working for this company, unless once again, you happen to be a turn-around expert.

Today there are an increasing number of legal problems for even the smallest company when it comes to the issue if harassment or abuse allegations. Make sure that you *investigate* any history of workplace violence, harassment or abuse before you make a commitment to work for any company. This is a very serious issue and can cause bucket loads of problems for a company and its owners and leadership. I cannot imagine anyone wanting to work in an environment where people look the other way when these types of actions occur. If you are now working in such an environment please take this message to heart immediately and take appropriate action to remove yourself from potential harm, and report the abusive conduct to people who will both take your seriously and who you believe will then take steps to remedy the situation. In addition to the obvious harm this kind of action causes the victims, the company will also suffer irreparable harm from a legal standpoint with any number of lawsuits. Remember that companies don't necessarily cause this type of action, its people that do the harm, but a company with a history of looking the other way and ignoring the problems is not where you want to work. The owners and top executives then become part of the problem.

NICHE ORIENTED BUSINESS MODEL

It's entirely possible that you're wondering what this means, and you would like to have an example of a niche oriented business model. First of all, a niche business is one that serves a very specific customer base with normally a very specific product or service. It would not be a company like Walmart or Amazon, because those companies serve a broad range of customers with a broad range of products and services (which could be a niche unto itself based on size and market share). It could be a small or medium size company that manufactures, as an example, a set of specific parts for Ford Motor Company to use in their assembly plants while building their final product, that being new cars and trucks. Many of these small manufacturers have only one customer such as Ford or General Motors or Chrysler.

So now you're wondering, okay what's the big deal here? How does this impact me when looking at an employer? The potential impact on you is that if there is a sudden financial downturn in the country and the automobile industry suffers a large drop in consumer demand for new cars and trucks, then your niche employer may very well have a dramatic drop in the need for the parts they manufacture. What comes next is usually a massive lay off of workers which could include you, or worse yet the company declaring bankruptcy or actually going out of business. Being employed by a niche company has a certain degree of risk by virtue of the lack of diversification of its products and services. I'm not saying don't take a job with a company like this, but to just *be aware* of the potential risks of doing so.

You might think that McDonald's has a niche type business model; you know - it's just a burger joint. I can agree on one hand that they do serve a particular niche audience, that being people pressed for time and looking for value. On the other hand I would disagree because McDonald's in particular is always looking to tweak their menu with new items and new versions of old items so that they don't become too much of a niche business. Their objective is to keep current customers coming back more often and to also keep adding more new customers, and they can achieve both by consistently *reinventing* their menu options. That strategy keeps them on the *cutting edge* of their industry and propels them to a continued environment of increased revenues and profits. For current and potential employees that means a higher degree of probability for job stability.

AGING EQUIPMENT, FACILITIES AND STAFF

This may be the easiest part of your overall external *analysis* of your employer, mainly because all you have to do is use your eyesight. Many companies of all shapes, sizes and industries will, over a period of time, make the decision to skimp here and there on maintaining equipment, updating equipment and replacing equipment. They do this to retain as much of their earnings as possible short term and to prolong expensive replacements for as long as possible. If you pull into a parking lot and see a bunch of old equipment, old cars or old trucks you will be able to tell very quickly that this company may not actually be doing as well financially as they might say they are. Be careful with expecting too much in this kind of situation.

You might also see this same scenario as you examine the outside of their facility and also the inside of their facility. If the outside looks anything like the equipment in the parking lot, you can pretty much assume that the same postpone tactics are being employed throughout the company. Then when you walk inside the facility you will most likely see the same thing - walls that need a fresh coat of paint, old furniture, old computers and copy machines, and pictures on the walls that look like they were put up there fifty years ago. These are all signs of an aging workplace, which may mean that there are some financial issues that you should be concerned about.

Next, as you walk through the facility, if all of a sudden you get the feeling that you're touring an old folk's home this might be your final wake up call to seriously consider working for another company. This is not to say that older people don't have enormous value in a company. They in fact do have an extraordinary amount of value because of their experience and tenure with the company. The issue is more one of - do you see yourself working in an environment where most of the people are the same relative age as your grandparents? Maybe you do, maybe you don't. All of these signals can be seen with your very own eyes, so you can be certain that this kind of company is one that dwells on the past more so than the future. It also means that this company may be steep in tradition rather than innovation. You will have to make your own determination as to whether you can fit into this kind of internal culture of this company for yourself.

You may also feel that because of the aging workforce that there may be little room for short term advancement opportunity.

DEAD END ADVANCEMENT POTENTIAL

If you talk with enough past employees, current employees, vendors and customers you will perhaps find out that there are a lot of family members working for the company. If there are, as an example, twenty people in the whole company and eight of them are family members of the owner/founder, you can be fairly certain that those family members are going to get the promotion opportunities before you will. That means there is dead end advancement potential, unless of course you find a way to start dating one of the kids and later get married to them. Then you become one of the family members! This of course is not a course of action that I recommend at all, but yes, it has happened this way in the past at any number of companies. If you are an aggressive person with an aspiration for more and more opportunity then this kind of company is probably not for you.

If on the other hand the company has five hundred employees and the number of family members is eight as it was in the above example, then your potential for advancement is significantly better. In the end you have to make your own determination of what you see and what you can live with both short term and long term. Use every resource possible to get the skinny on the internal familial dynamics of the company before you make the decision to join them. In this next chapter we will be examining the internal cultures that you may find as you enter the workforce.

CHAPTER THREE
SURVIVING THE INTERNAL CULTURE OF THE COMPANY

The internal culture of a company can be described as the "vibe" that you see, hear and sense as an employee. As an example, the culture can be open and inviting, warm and engaging, and very much team oriented. On the other hand the internal culture can be closed and distant, cold and uninviting, and very much me, me, me, it's all about me oriented.

Your current or future employer could be ripe with nepotism, which means you end up fighting for your survival against the owner or manager hiring and promoting family members over you, and doing so with blatant disregard for your feelings or your value. Your company can have an internal culture that is bureaucratic or one that is autocratic or one that is collaborative. Maybe you and your work will be appreciated and done so openly, or on the other hand, you and your work will be taken for granted.

I had a boss one time, who did manage to offer a congratulatory message when there was success to be recognized, but right after the short lived kudos he sent a shit missile across my bow, something along the lines of - well that's great news, Jim, but it's also old news; what have you done for me lately? - So much for allowing me to enjoy my moment of achievement. In reality it would have been far better if there had been no recognition, because in the end all it did was frustrate the hell out of me. It didn't motivate me to do something even greater in the future. What it did was to demoralize me. Trust me when I say this - that is not what you want to do to employees and that is not how employees want to be treated.

Maybe you will notice that your employer has an internal culture similar to the reality television show *Survivor*. It's everyone in it for themselves and the general consensus of the group is to kill or be killed (by the way I do not mean that literally). It is survival of the fittest by any and all means possible. In this kind of environment you will find some unscrupulous people who may very well do just about anything to get ahead. They may seem to be your friend but in reality they are sharks and they are after your blood (again, I do not mean this literally). If there's a promotion to be had they want it, and they want it bad enough to walk all over you to get there. This kind of internal culture is generally created by the leader because that's the kind of competitive atmosphere they desire. Unfortunately what they see as competitive spirit often ends up being cutthroat in nature. It ends up to be cage fighting without the mixed martial arts. Is that an environment you want to work in? Would you not want to find that out before you accept a job with this type of company? Of course you would. My advice to you is to stay away from these types of companies and those kinds of people.

The internal culture of a company can be inspirational for you or it could be a complete disaster for you. In the following subtitles we will examine a number of internal culture environments that you will want to *pay close attention* to and to be very *wary* of as your begin your journey, be it with a family owned company or even a publicly traded or privately held company.

GOOD OLD BOYS CLUB

The good old boys club on one hand is just what it sounds like - a fraternity type environment where the guys rule the roost and in so doing they revert back to collegiate type days when all they did was drink, chase women and cause trouble. Another example of a good old boys club would be a company where in fact the men are clearly in charge; first, because there are very few women, and second because most of the men are graybeards. In other words they're all old timers who love their buddy-buddy camaraderie type environment. Either way, unless you're a relative of one of the good old boys or a college friend of one of the good old boys, you will most definitely be on the outside looking in, with almost zero chance for advancement potential. And if you're a female it's far worse, because you will never be accepted into the inner circle of power and influence.

I knew someone who once worked for a company that was very much like the first type of good old boys club that I noted here. They told me there were companywide meetings and conventions held in nice resort type environments in Florida, Arizona, Hawaii and many other places just like them. Evidently, and far too often, the good old boys would stay out too late at night, drink far too much, show up for meetings half in the bag, or late, or not at all. It was equated to being back in college and basically focusing all thoughts and actions on when and where the next party was going to be held. Getting anything of consequence done from a business perspective was really a total waste of time. Females were not a welcome sight unless it involved the good old boys going to strip clubs. Company owners and offspring turned their heads and basically wrote the entire meeting off as boys will be boys - oh well they would say, the next meeting we'll pay closer attention to the business elements and try to tone down the party atmosphere. Yeah right! That was total bullshit. Rumor had it that some of the managers and owners were out doing things they shouldn't have been doing either, like maybe hooking up outside their marriage (now that is strictly a rumor mind you). Is this the kind of internal culture where you want to work?

This type of internal culture can be found more in certain industries and certain companies within those industries. It is more prevalent in male dominated industries such as trucking, transportation, logistics, warehousing, railroads and skilled labor, among many others. It is important for you to *inspect what you expect*, meaning that you need to *do your homework* about your employer's internal culture to make sure that it will fit with your personal expectations once you are actually there as an employee. Another issue to be aware of as you study your next or current employer is whether you are in an arena where the company is in limbo, in other words, going nowhere fast.

STAGNATION

A company that has an owner or leader with no aspirations for continued growth and profitability is one to *be wary of as you examine* your future employment. Let's say that you are thinking about accepting a job at a local pizza shop. This shop has been in existence at its current location for over ten years. During that time their revenues and profits have been very steady, with little growth and little decline. The owner has indicated that they have no intention or interest in expanding beyond this one store. They are comfortable with what they have and where they are in life. This would be an example of a stagnant environment. In essence there will be little if any potential for you to grow in your job or in your income. You will be mired in repetitive work every day you're there. Is this going to be fulfilling for you longer term?

There might, however, be somewhat of a silver lining in working for this type of company. It may prove to be an excellent training ground for your next job and your career. Let's take the same example I used above. You decide to take the job in this stagnant pizza parlor with the *thought in mind* that you are going to do your best to learn every facet of the business. You do this so that you can, at some point in time, go on to maybe open your own pizza shop, or maybe go to work for one of the large pizza franchise type stores as a manager. These are admirable intentions and certainly good reasons to go to work, at least temporarily, in a stagnant environment. At the very least you need to *recognize* these types of companies for what they are and for what they might be able to do for you as time goes on.

Study your employer carefully to find the right fit for you. Two other internal cultures to be concerned about are nepotism and patronage. In both circumstances you will find yourself rowing against the current for most of your time there. These cultures are both entrenched with loyalties and friendships that end up being far more important than other employee characteristics such as capability or expertise.

NEPOTISM

An internal culture with nepotism as an inherent foundation is one where family ties are what matters the most. It is one where the founder, owner or manager is predisposed to the notion that their children or spouse, or other relatives, will eventually rise to the top echelons of the company. In this type of scenario there is almost zero chance that you or anyone else not in the familial tree will ever get to the point of leading this company. That's okay as long as you are *aware* of that prospect *before* you enter the arena. Joining such a company without realizing the nepotism issue ahead of time will tend to frustrate you over time as you come to the realization that you will never get to the top, and maybe never get promoted, if that's even on your radar.

Companies that thrive on nepotism create situations where the owner or manager's offspring or extended family members ascend to positions of authority without necessarily earning that promotion. They have not risen through the ranks so-to-speak, but instead are anointed by the owner or manager as being ready to lead. In many cases the offspring are not ready for this next step in leadership, and therefore they tend to stumble their way through a learning curve that may prove to be difficult for them as well as for the employees reporting to them. This can be extremely challenging for you as an employee if you encounter this type of situation in your own employment journey.

You can learn to recognize these scenarios by *studying* the executive ranks of a company. If you see a last name at the top of the organization chart and then see that same last name in several other spots on that same chart, then you can come to the conclusion that there is a high likelihood of nepotism being prevalent at that company. There are other inherent challenges that come with this type of internal culture, one of them being a clash between offspring for the heir apparent job once the owner retires. This can be especially nasty if the siblings are more rivals than collaborators.

I know someone who worked in this kind of culture for a time and they witnessed first-hand the underlying negativity that can erupt when offspring become rivals. The siblings start to create their own followers, their own gang of supporters who become bound to one respective person over the other. What follows is a fractured company structure, with one group of employees having allegiance to the owner, another group more supportive of one of the siblings, and yet one other group of employees serving the other sibling. Can you imagine the uncertainty of those internal dynamics? The company becomes unfocused on the overall objectives and instead becomes fractured with internal dissent and at times, creates open hostility.

In this company they witnessed the management doing what you may think is unthinkable - stoking the fires of siblings to see who would come out on top. It became somewhat of a scenario out of the olden days of the Roman Coliseum, where gladiators would be pitted against one another for a fight to the death, all for the amusement of the emperor and the general public. Was it really necessary to pit the siblings against one another in some public display of survival of the fittest? The drama between owner and siblings was disheartening at the very least and *completely counterproductive* in the end. This kind of situation can be very difficult for you as a new employee and even more so if you have been with your employer for a period of time.

Perhaps this kind of culture becomes less of a problem in companies that are considerably larger in scope and size. Let's say that you go to work for a large car dealership that sells multiple brands, makes and models, and one that also has five different locations. You learn that the owner is nearing retirement age and that there are two siblings, both of whom work there, but neither of whom have expressed an interest in taking over the full reins of the company. In this situation you at least have more of a chance to earn your way to promotions because of the apparent lack of interest or capability of the siblings. You actually have a fighting chance to show your leadership potential and get ahead.

Again, working in this kind of internal culture can be challenging at best. You need to pay attention to the details and find out as much information as you can before you go to work there. Another potential problem is patronage.

PATRONAGE

When you think of patronage the first thing that might come to mind is politics because that is where patronage is openly and unapologetically rampant. If you've ever worked for a campaign in a serious manner then you might have done so with some degree of hope that if your candidate won then you might have been rewarded for your efforts with a position in that candidate's governmental administration. That reward of sorts for your supportive efforts is called patronage.

In a company environment patronage is more closely tied to people that the owner or management leader knows on a personal basis, but those people are not family members. If they were family members it would be referred to as nepotism. Patronage refers in this case to preferential treatment being given to close personal friends or supporters of the owner or manager. You as an employee have the same general problem with either of these internal cultures because one is not too much of a difference from the other in terms of what they mean to you. In either case the owner or manager is likely to give new job opportunities or promotions or pay raises to people who are either related or people who are close friends or confidants.

There is one major difference between nepotism and patronage and simply put, that is - blood is thicker than water. The chances of the owner or manager firing a family member are much less than the chances of the owner or manager firing a friend. Patronage rewards friendship and/or support, and the level of engagement is much looser than in family relationships. You might find yourself being in this situation one day where you could get a job at some company where one of your high school or college buddies now owns. Your friendship might help get you the job, but it will not help you keep the job. You too will be expected to toe the line and achieve your specific job objectives. If not you will be out on your ass sooner than you think.

Nevertheless patronage is an internal culture that can cause you more grief than you want. As an example, let's say that you end up reporting to one of the owner or manager's friends. This friend, your new boss, is a bit of a square peg in a round hole in that they are really not qualified for the job they now have. You begin to quasi tutor this new boss, helping them get accustomed to the new job and helping them resolve some issues. Then one day disaster hits. Something goes wrong. Your boss - the owner's friend - is the one responsible for the problem, but they end up blaming you. You become the scapegoat, the employee who is left walking out the exit with a resounding - don't let the door hit you in the ass on your way out. Ah, you now realize the relationship importance between owner or manager and friend, as opposed to owner and employee. You stand no chance of survival because the owner will almost always side with the friend, as it would also be between owner and family member. You will the odd person out.

Another aspect of patronage is when the owner or manager gets completely bamboozled by some smooth talking, snake charming bullshit artist who one day shows up out of nowhere. Maybe, as in the case of a leader I once knew, this happened one day when they were shoe shopping in New York City. The manager was shopping for a new pair of shoes because there was an important sales call the next day. The shoe salesperson overwhelmed the manager with their professionalism, product knowledge and charisma. The leader hired the salesperson on the spot for a management position in a different part of the country, requiring the new employee to relocate from New York City to Houston,

Texas. They both left the store feeling like they had a great day, giving one another hugs and high fives. The manager promised to stay in touch.

So where's the problem you are now asking? One problem was that the salesperson doesn't know squat about the business; another problem was that Houston is a far cry from New York in terms of cultural; yet another problem was that the other employees in Houston felt blindsided because they were now reporting to someone they know nothing about and who knows nothing about their local business market. In fact, several of the people in the Houston office were hoping for the promotion that the new person just got handed out of nowhere. This is an example of patronage based on a personal relationship or encounter. In the end none of it worked out for anyone. It was the wrong hire for the wrong reason, at the wrong time, at and for the wrong place. Nothing good came out of this hire. The new manager eventually quit because of the cultural differences and the employee discontent, and the Houston branch lost two of their best salespeople over the fact that they were passed over for the managerial promotion that the new person got. This is an example of how things can go haywire by virtue of an internal culture built on patronage hiring practices.

Obviously it will be important for you to make an attempt to in*vestigate* the internal culture of your current or future employer. You will also want to *find out* if your employer has a culture that has tendencies to disregard your opinions and value, or as an alternative, if they are warm, welcoming, engaging and always open to your ideas.

SHUT UP AND WORK

This kind of culture is exactly what it sounds like. You are a means to an end, a robot that is expected to do exactly as you are told, a piece of meat to be devoured if necessary, a victim of collateral damage when and if disaster strikes. Your importance on a scale of one to ten is clearly closer to one. You are there to serve the master, not to talk, not to offer opinions or advice, and certainly not to ever question the master's wisdom or intellect. You are there to work, period, so just shut up and work. Sound like a fun place to work? I'm fairly sure you are shaking your head in sheer disbelief that this kind of environment even exists. Trust me; there are lots of companies like this, owned or managed by tyrants and dictators who masquerade as leaders.

Early in my career I did work for a company that had such a leader. The environment was very strict in terms of expectations and output. There was little if any value put on my own job aspirations. I was there to work and to make a lot more money for the owner. It was more like indentured servitude than being an employee. As I sit here thinking about this short lived, past experience of mine, I am hard pressed to reconcile with myself as to why I stayed as an employee for as long as I did. I think perhaps it was because the owner changed their persona when it was convenient to do so; when it was expedient for the moment in time. They were capable of being one kind of person one day and another kind of person the next day; a Jekyll and Hyde type of persona. I was always trying to figure out which person would show up for work the next day. In the end their true color would always emerge the victor; the tyrant would always win. The employee - me - would always lose. This is not the kind of environment you want to work in.

This kind of internal culture can be found in large companies and in small companies. More often than not, the smaller the company the more likelihood there is to run across the dictator type of owner or manager. Large companies need a lot more employees and the owner or manager does not interact with as many as they might in a smaller company. The owner or manager's success will come more from the success of the employees than their own. In smaller companies the owner or manager is more likely to be engaged at every level or facet of the company. They are inclined to be way more hands-on than hands-off, and they engage with every single employee. By doing so they are likely to be more autocratic - it's my way or the highway - you don't like it, then you can leave they say. That becomes their mantra, their way of managing their business because they need to keep a firm grip on everything that goes on, and that grip on things includes you.

You might run into a situation where the owner or manager starts dictating not only what you can and cannot do at work, they might also start to tell you what you can and cannot do outside of work. Maybe they start to tell you that there are certain people you should not hang out with or have as friends. Maybe they tell you that you should not be going out to a particular bar or restaurant because that's where they go, and they don't want to be seen with their employees after work hours. Maybe they start to tell you should be going to their church or going to their doctor or banking at their bank. They get to the point where they are basically telling you how to run your life. This can be a very demeaning work environment and worse yet, it can be extremely damaging to your personal life and psyche. If you find yourself in this kind of workplace I would strongly encourage you to depart as soon as you are able to find a new job.

We will next explore a number of internal cultures that are a one-hundred and eighty degree contrast from this previous one, and these are the types of environments you should be looking to embrace for your longer term employment.

INVITING AND ENGAGING

On day one of your employment you are greeted with open arms by the owner or management and later by everyone else in the company. You immediately sense an aura of happy, friendly people, all of whom embrace you as one of theirs. On day two, three, four, eight and ninety-eight you feel and sense the same things you did on day one. You realize that day one was not an anomaly. The stuff on day one was the real deal, not some bullshit façade that was orchestrated to wean you into the group. It's not a cult and it's not a club; it's a company that operates as though they were a family. In fact, it might be a family owned business, but in this case you realize that the ownership genuinely cares about their employees and treats them as though they were family. Sit back and smile, for you have found nirvana.

You find that the owner talks to everyone almost on a daily basis. I can relate to this type of environment because in my own days as a leader I espoused to a management philosophy of *MBWA - management by walking around*. I found that far too many leaders led by sitting behind their desk. They would read reports, stare at their computer, and have employees come into their office for updates. I found that employees liked it far better if I went to their place, their desk, or their office to engage in conversation. The kind of owner or manager I'm talking about here is the one who leads by walking around, not by dictates ordered from behind their desk or through emails. This is the kind of owner or leader who is engaging and personable, who cares about their employees as people not just as instruments of business. This is the kind of owner or manager who asks for your opinion because they actually want it. This is the kind of person you want to work for and the kind of internal culture where you will flourish in your career.

JAMES W. BENDER

APPRECIATION

Let's say that regardless of what company you work for, and regardless of what your position is at your company, you work hard at your job and be the best that you can be for your employer. To your complete delight you find that your boss - and maybe that's the owner - slaps you gently and kindly on the back, gives you high fives, and genuinely praises you for your efforts. Your work is appreciated and you find yourself immersed in an environment of satisfaction. You never find yourself in a situation where you are wondering how your work is perceived. Your boss tells you and does so frequently. This is the kind of workplace where employees can flourish with excitement and achievement. It is where employees feel emotionally compelled to work harder and more efficiently. It is a workplace where people are happy and where everyone truly feels a sense of *camaraderie*.

In all honesty a lot of people have never worked at any company where this kind of environment existed. Their employment history is unfortunately filled with employers, bosses and owners who for whatever reason felt it necessary to always keep them and other employees on pins and needles at all times. They followed a managerial philosophy where they wanted their employees to feel a sense of uncomfortableness with their jobs, never knowing for sure on any given day whether their days were numbered or whether their future was solidified. I have never personally understood this philosophy and I understand it less today. In my opinion people excel in an environment where there is *genuineness* in the way they are treated, and one where they are treated fairly and honestly at all times. People who worry about their job prospects are far more likely to be employees who are constantly looking for another job at another company.

Look for employers who have an internal culture that is filled with happy employees who are appreciated for the work they do. You should also look for a company that prides itself on having a team oriented environment, where success comes about by people working together.

COLLABORATIVE

Imagine that you walk in the doors of your new employer on day one. Your eyes and ears are searching for clues to substantiate the decision that you made to accept a job with this company. If you see people walking alone or sitting alone, you may think nothing of it. On the flip side you may see people gathered in small groups, or even larger groups. Not only do you see these gatherings taking place but you hear excitement in people's voices. So what does all this mean to you?

Employees walking, sitting and working alone may very well suggest that you are entering an internal culture where everyone is on their own, doing their own job and not caring very much about each other. Employees walking together, sitting together in groups and talking with each other with passion in their voices might mean that you are entering an internal culture of employee collaboration. This latter kind of environment is one where *teamwork* is encouraged. It's not an arena of survival of the fittest; it's one that is caring, nurturing, and encouraging. It's where employees work together to solve problems and brainstorm issues. By working in a collective manner they achieve through and with one another, rather than as lone ranger types. This kind of internal culture is filled with fun, excitement, learning and celebration. If you don't like being on a team then this company might not be your best fit.

JAMES W. BENDER

TEAM ORIENTED

A collaborative culture is one where employees engage in team oriented activities. They meet in groups to talk openly and freely about the business issues they are facing. They meet as cross functional groups so that they may include other departments or business areas, and solve problems for the benefit of the entire company and not just one singular business unit.

Years ago I took a job with a privately held company as a new executive leader where I found an internal culture of suspicion, disconnect, distrust and acrimony. The executive team all seemed to be running for higher office and that me-first aspiration from each of them resulted in an environment where decisions were made departmentally rather than collectively for the overall good of the company. One department head would issue a new policy without talking to the other department heads about how that new policy might impact the other departments and their respective areas of responsibility. It was no wonder that this particular company was having serious financial problems. People in high positions were acting as selfish individuals as opposed to collaborative teammates. It was a problem that I focused on fixing immediately. No more unilateral decisions were going to be made in the future. I let them know that any and all decisions of significant financial impact were going to be made as a group until such time that I thought they fully recognized the importance of doing so.

Of course I also found out that each department head had their own direct reports functioning the same way that they were. It was a sort of cancer that had grown throughout the entire organization. It had become an arena of survival of the fittest.

SURVIVAL OF THE FITTEST

This kind of internal culture is the exact opposite of collaborative and team oriented. It sounds exactly like the one I just referenced in the last section. I believe I already mentioned that there are some bosses and owners who purposely cultivate a survival of the fittest environment. They want to pit people against one another to see who comes out on top. I have personally witnessed this type of culture more than once in my career. None of the circumstances were comfortable for me and certainly not for most other employees. There were of course the typical piranha types who were all too eager to feed on others to get what they wanted. I guess that's what the owner wanted, but it sure as hell didn't achieve any tangible business results for the company. This type of internal culture is self-defeating and chaotic. It results in an aura of uncomfortable distrust, where people will actually try their best to make others look bad in the eyes of the boss or owner.

I've seen circumstances in the past where one employee would openly blame another employee for a business error or bad judgment call. There were other survivor-oriented employees that would make that case behind closed doors to the owner or manager, whispering in their ear as thought they were passing state secrets that could be deemed treasonous. *Beware the wolf in sheep's clothing!* The piranhas will look nice and talk friendly, but once you are out of eyesight or earshot they will cut you to ribbons. They are the type of people who will pander the owner or manager.

PANDERING THE BOSS

These are employers commonly known as suck-ups and ass kissers, and some of them do far worse. These are the type of employees who will tell the boss or owner anything the boss or owner wants to hear. Whatever the boss says this type of employee will agree with and they will do so time and time again. You will be able to spot them easily because they will have their head stuck so far up the boss's ass that all you will see is neck and body. They will constantly be running in and out of the owners' office doing and saying whatever they can to better their own position in the boss's eyes. They will also be all too happy to mention you as often as possible as an albatross within the organization; someone who therefore should be terminated as soon as possible. If you are someone who is smarter than they are and functioning at a high level within the company, then you are in real danger of being sabotaged by the panderer.

This type of internal company culture is all too common. People are, after all, human beings with lots of faults and frail inadequacies. Owners and managers too are human beings and when they are in a position of power and influence that means that they may cherish being loved and adored by people beneath them in status and rank. Now I don't necessarily mean to say that all employees behave in this way; in fact very few of them do. Nor do I mean to say that all bosses and owners behave in a godlike fashion. However, the fact of the matter is that this type of culture does exist, and you as a new or current employee need to make a quick *determination* if this kind of environment the right place for you to work and find success.

Pander means to gratify or indulge someone's desires for attention or needs. These needs can simply be idol-like in nature, or they can be immoral in nature. Telling the owner or manager everything they want or need to hear so that they are constantly being told how great they are, is pandering to their egotistical needs and desires. Committing immoral acts to satisfy the boss's needs may fall into an entirely different category of pandering behavior. An example might be to help the owner or manager "cook the books" so-to-speak, where in a sense you are indulging the boss's desire to report inaccurate financial results for immoral and illegal purposes. Another example might involve sexual gratification and favors in order to satisfy the boss's needs. These are examples of internal company cultures that are toxic to employees in general. If you see these things taking place you should start looking for another place to hang your hat.

We will now take a look at an example of a wonderful internal culture to find for your longer term employment enjoyment and career success, one where new ideas are cherished and where everyone is appreciated for their innovation.

INNOVATION ORIENTED AND AN IDEA FACTORY

This type of internal company culture is one where new ideas are never frowned upon or discarded. This culture is generally driven by the owner or manager's recognition that the world of business never stands still. As an old boss of mine used to say - *you either eat dust or you make dust* - meaning that you are either content with a stagnating environment where nothing new gets accomplished and the competition is kicking your ass, or you are constantly generating new and unique ways of doing business in order to stay ahead of your competitors. Companies that engage in innovation and progress as their mainstay themes and mission are very likely to have a consistent growth curve and future trend line. This type of internal culture is one that will benefit the employees in terms of their future opportunity, their future compensation, their future stability, and their future enjoyment of the job and company culture.

When you think of Apple or Google or Facebook or Amazon or Tesla, do you think of these companies as eating dust or making dust? When you think of Sears or General Electric or Lehman Brothers or Toys "R" Us or Enron or WorldCom, do you think of these companies as eating dust or making dust? Some of the ones listed in the latter group are already dead and buried in dust. So what do you think the first grouping has in common? The answer is that they thrive on innovation. They thrive on *breaking down barriers.* They thrive on being *disruptors* in their own industry. The only way they can achieve this distinction is by creating and maintaining an internal culture that has as its main engine of success a driving need and desire for new ideas from their employees. They also achieve this internal culture by focusing on the unknowns in their business and in the world and in life in general. They look for things that cannot be seen today because they don't exist today.

Some years ago a guy by the name of Donald Rumsfeld, Secretary of Defense at the time under President George W. Bush, was holding a news conference wherein he unleashed a series of baffling statements regarding the future. The press corps and media mocked him as someone who was weird, arrogant and nonsensical. His statement at the time went something like this - *there are things that we know that we know, there are things that we know that we don't know, and then there are things that we don't know that we don't know.* The people listening at the time of the press conference were stunned, shaking their heads thinking that Rumsfeld had finally lost his mind. They thought it was yet another end-around answer from the Pentagon about the war prospects on the horizon.

The fact is that the last part of his statement about not knowing what we don't know is what is at the very heart of research and development, think tank strategic planning, war games planning, space exploration, and companies that are driven by unlocking the unknowns of life. Seeking the unknowns is what drives companies to create an environment where they make dust and bury their competitors. Does working in an idea factory sound like fun to you? It might if you are someone who relishes a challenge. It might not if you are someone who is more of an implementer than a strategist. In any case it pays for you to *recognize* this type of internal culture before you take a job at one of these innovation oriented companies.

You will also want to dive into whether your employer has a secretive internal culture or whether it thrives on having an open book environment.

SECRETIVE

If you stop and think about some examples of a secretive internal culture you will probably come up with various government type institutions and places like the Pentagon, the Central Intelligence Agency, the Situation Room at the White House, the National Security Agency, and various military intelligence agencies. Step into any one of these locations and you will probably hear a pin drop and all eyes will be on you. There will not much talking going on and your arrival, even if expected, produces uncertainty at best and paranoia at worst among any and all people present in the room. These organizations deal in secrecy all day, every day. There are even secrets among the secret keepers that other secret keepers don't know about. The day to day operational guideline is probably something close to this - if you don't know the person you see or meet inside our community then don't talk to that person without proper approval from someone with a higher level of top secret security clearance.

I do not believe that you will encounter this type of secrecy in your place of employment unless you go to work for a government contractor that is involved, as an example, with building military equipment, satellite equipment or other types of surveillance equipment. For the most part

I think most of you will be a far cry from that level of secrecy. There are however any number of business circumstances that will and do require a degree of secrecy. Most of that will originate from legal departments that want to protect patents, trademarks and other types of proprietary assets, all of which have significant value to a company. You may even be required to sign a confidentiality agreement or a non-disclosure agreement to ensure that you recognize and agree to the nature of the secretive environment in which you work.

I am really not talking about any of the above situations when I mention secrecy. I am talking more about a small company situation where the owner or manager creates an internal culture of distrust among their employees. Everything will be a secret - revenue numbers, profit numbers, client satisfaction numbers, turnover numbers, law suit numbers, compensation details; virtually everything will be a secret because that's the way the boss wants it. They want to make sure that no one other than themselves knows any of the details of the company. That is a secretive company, produced and directed by the owner or manager. Employees do not talk about these secrets because first, they don't know the actual details, and second because the owner or manager may very well fire them on the spot. In other words there is an underlying element of fear that resonates throughout the company. Think this is the kind of place you want to work?

OPEN BOOK ENVIRONMENT

Here is the exact opposite of the above situation. Let's say you walk in to your new employer on day one and as you are greeted and led throughout the facility to meet everyone, you notice color coded charts and graphs hanging all over the walls. It turns out that these banners and such depict the company's performance in a variety of categories. Some of the categories are daily, some are weekly, some are monthly, some are departmentalized, some may even be individualized, and others are annual.

After you settle in to your job for several days you begin to receive email blasts from various internal departments that announce even more *performance* related results. You begin to get the feeling that this company has an internal culture where they want every single employee to know everything about how the company operates. This is a shining example of an open book environment. This can only happen if the owner or manager believes in this type of culture.

This type of open internal culture is good in many ways, especially because it can incentivize employees to *work together to achieve better results*. How you ask? It's difficult for employees to strive for higher targets if they don't already know where things stand on a current basis. Only by having the current benchmarks and setting higher targets can the employees work efficiently and successfully toward achieving the desired results. On the other hand this type of open culture can be bad in some ways. One of those ways can occur when employees of the company leave and go to work for a different company that operates in the same basic industry. Since the people that leave the company know the strong points and weak points of their employer, they can then pass those things along to their new employer and provide important information from a competitive perspective. This information could weaken their previous employer. Of course if everyone had to sign a confidentiality agreement as a requirement of their initial employment then this issue may be diluted somewhat for a period of time.

Generally speaking an open internal culture can be far more enjoyable and far more rewarding for employees. Think about almost any kind of athletic team and how they view their progress throughout a game. The players and coaches all know where things stand at any given time. The score is not a secret to anyone. All the competitors know what they have to do to beat the competition. It is an open book environment. Can you imagine a sports event where the scores would be held as secret information until the very end of the competition? Playing in a blind game would diminish the quality, intensity and meaning of the game for the players, the coaches and the fans. Again, the open book culture is the best way to go if you're looking at reasons to join a certain employer.

In the final pages of this chapter we will take a look at a couple different types of managerial environments that can have serious implications for employees as they make decisions on whether to join a new company or remain with a current company. The implications revolve around how much input employees have in these types of internal cultures and whether they can adapt to the different styles of leadership.

BUREAUCRATIC

This type of internal culture is rife with decision making roadblocks due in part to too many layers of management, a certain amount of abdication of authority by the owner or founder, and the underlying need to gain near universal consensus prior to any implementation choices. The main problem associated with this type of culture is that things take too long to get finalized and implemented, making it easier for competitors to leave them in the dust (recall the make dust or eat dust distinction in a previous heading). This can be frustrating for employees who desire a faster paced environment where opportunities are jumped on quickly in order to take advantage of time and circumstance.

I have had the opportunity in the past to engage with various non-profit organizations, most of which have the best of intentions. Many of these non-profits have an Executive Director, an employee staff, and a Board of Directors that has legal oversight responsibilities for the organization mission and results. I have seen far too many organization charts with far too many layers of management, and in some cases where there are only a few people that actually report directly to the Executive Director. The more layers of management that you find, the more difficult it can be to get decisions made in a timely fashion. The Executive Director typically will want as many opinions as possible. Why you might ask is that? There are two main reasons. One, the Executive Director wants a shield from the Board, meaning that they want to present things to the Board that has consensus from the majority of internal employees and other constituents. By driving consensus they operate with a shield of sorts from Board criticism. Two, the Executive Director is not the type of leader who has the managerial characteristics or internal fortitude to make decisions on their own, and the willingness to then live or die (so-to-speak) with the consequences.

I actually worked for someone who had the management tendency to need the opinions of every direct report before making a decision, and every time a decision was actually made the person made sure that their boss knew that the decision was made in unison and not as a singular choice. They made sure that their ass was protected in case the decision turned out to be the wrong one. This person always looked for the scapegoat prior to even needing a scapegoat. Working for this kind of leader is like trying to get Jell-O to stop jiggling. There is always a moving target and you can never get this person to commit to anything on their own. They can be very frustrating for you the employee and you can actually become their scapegoat if you're not careful.

An internal culture that is dependent upon some form of universal consensus and decision making is one that unnecessarily bogs the company down in indecision and creates a very slow moving environment. If you are an employee in this type of culture you too might get bogged down, tired and frustrated. You will be living the life of the proverbial hamster running on the wheel but going nowhere fast. If you're the type of person who wants a face paced culture then you better watch out for the overly bureaucratic workplace.

Of course you might also have the equally unpleasant experience of working in an autocratic internal culture where there is a king and everyone else is a peon.

AUTOCRATIC

The king that I am referring to is the owner or founder or top executive of a company. The peons are every other person who works for this company. There are two ways of doing things the king will announce - my way and the wrong way. They will add this statement - it's my way or the highway. You as an employee will in essence find yourself in an environment run by a dictator. Your opinion may be solicited or it may not be solicited. If you do come up with a good idea it will thereafter be the king's idea. Remember, you are a peon, someone who might be disregarded at will.

Of course I am exaggerating things just a tad here to make a point, but clearly an autocratic culture really is one where you do as you're told and where your ability to move up in the organization is almost entirely based on how much and how often you decide to suck up and kiss ass to the king or queen. If you're the kind of person who has no problem with being the king's or queen's servant, then you may very well succeed in this kind of internal culture. If you're a leader, and a decision maker, and someone who craves a position of importance, and one where you are valued, then you may be the odd person out in this type of company.

An autocratic culture can spell doom for the company if the dictator takes no direction or input from the employees. They can and will make decisions that are in their best interests. Employee interests will lag far behind, as will customer interests as well. Remember the story I mentioned previously about the owner of a company who announced that they wanted to provide services to every person in America, but only once? The leader of that company acted and behaved like a dictator, refusing to take advice and counsel from virtually anyone. This arrogant decision making style eventually required that the company file for bankruptcy protection, after which it was eventually sold for pennies on the dollar. I doubt that you want to work for a leader like that or a company managed by a dictator type personality. Remember, an autocratic internal culture is one built by the owner or founder or manager, not by the employees. Always keep an eye on the reputation of the owner or leader if you want to *make the right choices* about joining a company.

If your initial interview for a job is with the owner or top manager then you may very well be able to tell if the organization is run in an autocratic style. The owner or manager will come across as having little if any leeway if things don't go their way. You can try asking a question about how your opinions and suggestions would be welcomed at this company. If the owner or manager jumps out of their chair in a tantrum, or sits back in their chair as if to say how you dare ask that question, or stares a hole through you with daggers coming out of their eyes, then you know the answer to your query. You may as well just get up and leave unless you want to work somewhere where you are not really valued.

The ideal internal workplace culture is one where every employee is valued, where there are limited layers of management, where your suggestions are accepted willingly, where employees work together in a collaborative manner, where you feel like you belong, and where you find happiness, contentment and future opportunity. This kind of culture does exist, but you need to look hard to find it.

In this next chapter we will take a look at surviving the sustainability of a company. After all, if the company is not sustainable then you as an employee have limited employment stability or opportunity.

CHAPTER FOUR
DETERMINING THE SUSTAINABILITY OF THE COMPANY

Sustainability can have two different meanings or concepts with regard to companies. One has to do with how well a company is positioned to continue on into the future as a going concern, which might have a significant impact on your decision to join a new company or remain with your current employer. Will the company survive and if so for how long? Is the company secure enough in its leadership ranks to maintain its' value and competitiveness? Is the business model geared toward future customer demands? Will people keep buying the services or products of the company? Does the company have a solid financial position that will sustain it into the future? These are the types of things that I mean when I say company sustainability.

The second meaning of sustainability is the company's policy toward being environmentally friendly to its customers, suppliers and the ecosystem in general. This has to do with a company's green initiatives and containing any environmentally harmful aspects of their manufacturing or assembly processes, such as greenhouse gases. It relates to company policies regarding their recycling program and their reduction in the usage of paper, plastics and other environmentally harmful items. I will examine this particular definition of sustainability in one of the subchapters later on, but for the most part this chapter as a whole deals with how well a company is positioned for continued existence and success.

Sustainability is an especially important consideration for employees who decide to work for any type of company, but especially for a family owned or controlled company or a newly established company. A lot of family owned companies might be start-ups, meaning they are just starting their new company from scratch. You will want to know that 33% of start-ups fail within two years and 50% fail within five years. Only 10% of start-ups make it past ten years. Remember the dot-com boom followed by the dot-com bust years ago? That was an example of how difficult it is to determine the real viability of a company that just got started from scratch, and that's regardless of the amount of investment capital that may be infused into the opportunity. You don't want to get confused or misdirected when you look at the equity participants, as many of them may be well known names and players. So you will want to do your homework when considering a job with a new start-up to make an educated guess as to their future prospects for success. You want to analyze their leadership, their market segment and their financial wherewithal, as these are three indicators of sustainability.

If you are specifically considering going to work for a family owned company you will want to know if they have a succession plan in place, especially if the owner or original founder is older and getting ready to retire. Statistics indicate that only 20% of family owned companies have a detailed, written succession plan in place. What happens when the owner decides to retire and there's no succession plan in place? The owner then decides to either sell the company or just close the doors, both of which could spell an iffy future for you the employee.

You may also want to consider which of the four business life cycles your company is at when you decide to join the company or even if you're already employed by a going concern. Is the company in a start-up stage, or is it in a growth stage, or is it in a maturity/renewal stage, or is it in a decline stage? Each of these stages carries a unique set of challenges and opportunities for employees.

The start-up stage has a certain amount of risk for employees because of the failure rate mentioned previously. Work for one of these companies and your tenure could be short lived. The growth stage could be a very exciting and opportunistic time for employees because the company is presumably past the risk factor stage and is now engaged in successful growth and profitability. This is a time for employees to flourish in their careers. The maturity/renewal stage is one where the company has had much success to date but now finds itself flapping its wings so-to-speak and never quite getting off the ground. Their growth has stagnated, their competition is gaining headway, and they are now fighting every day just to keep their head above water. They are somewhat in limbo and they have decided and actually need to reinvent themselves. This carries a degree of risk for employees because company owners and managers will tend to eliminate expense by first downsizing the workforce. The riskiest stage is of course the decline stage because the company has, for whatever reasons, started to have a steady decline in revenue and profit, which can then lead to the sale of the business or outright failure. The trick here is to recognize which stage your employer is in before you get there. One of the ways you do that is by examining their growth history and patterns.

GROWTH HISTORY AND PATTERNS

Any company's business sustainability is highly dependent upon revenue patterns and overall growth. The ideal revenue pattern is one that shows a steady level of revenue improvement year over year. This will typically mean that customers are happy with the product or service and there is credible evidence of repeat business. There will also be evidence of new customer growth, which is in addition to the added buying patterns of current customers. Your objective as an employee is to not only ferret out the patterns but to also find out how and why the patterns are occurring.

You will hopefully recall that I mentioned previously the potential of revenue increases due to a pattern of discounting the company's prices. This can be a misleading scenario that you will want to analyze. Generally speaking your best employer fit for the future is one where the revenue improvement numbers are from increased business transactions, not just increased revenue dollars. More transactions mean that customers are really buying at a higher new order pace rather than simply a higher dollar volume pace. Let's face it, if customers are buying at a higher order pace, then the company knows they have a solid market position, and with a solid market position they can then raise their pricing to a market bearing level that achieves client retention objectives. A company's customer acquisition expense and growth is far more economical via client retention than new client development.

So I've mentioned the ideal revenue pattern for a company, what about the not so ideal patterns. What do they mean to you? A revenue pattern that dramatically spikes up and then dramatically spikes down over multiple years is one to be concerned about as it relates to your future. Another pattern of concern would be one where there is inverse revenue generation, meaning that income is going south rather than north. Maybe there are good reasons for the decline in revenues, but you will definitely want to determine the causes of such an outcome before taking a new job at a company with this kind of pattern. Again, these types of negative patterns could be a service problem, a quality problem and maybe even a leadership problem. You need to be the one that makes that determination, and to then decide what kind of impact that might have on the company's sustainability.

Your ideal employment opportunity for the future is with a company that displays a consistent history of revenue and profit improvement or one where there is an extremely strong balance sheet with plenty of cash availability. This means *stability and dependability* for you as an employee, both very important considerations for longer term employment opportunity.

PROFITABILITY

You as an employee will want to know if your company is generating profits. What happens when a company ceases to make a profit? They may survive temporarily, but if that kind of result occurs year after year or frequently then the handwriting may be on the wall for a bankruptcy, a sale, or the company going out of business. Very few owners or private equity managers will continue to throw good money after bad, meaning that if profitability is nonexistent, they are unlikely to put more money into a business that is using more money than it takes in. If you see this type of environment you need to consider making an immediate career move before you end up without a job, or even worse, you end up being tagged as part of the problem at your company. Remember, in most situations in life and in business you're looked at as either part of the solution or part of the problem.

Perhaps even more important than profits is the cash flow situation at any company. It is virtually impossible for any company to operate without enough cash to pay their bills and their employees. Let's say you notice that your company has seen an increase in revenues but you also see that the increase is from customers who are taking a lot longer to pay their invoices. Your company was used to getting payment within a ten day time frame. A relatively large but new client has made a commitment to pay within fifteen days but it turns out they're paying the vast majority of their invoices almost forty-five to sixty days later. Your company has a fairly slim profit margin, meaning in this example that out of every dollar of revenue they take in, ninety-five cents goes to vendors, suppliers, contractor and employees. It turns out that most of these payments are made within two weeks of the work taking place, so all of a suddenly the company is paying out money faster than they are collecting it. A constant diet of this scenario and this type of customer is a recipe for a cash flow disaster. In this kind of situation it is typical for the company to either borrow money to float cash needs, file for bankruptcy protection or just close their doors entirely. None of these alternatives are good news for you the employee.

A friend of mine joined a company many years ago that was losing money at the time. To be precise they were running at a 106% operating margin, which meant they were losing $.06 on every $1.00 of revenue. Clearly they were in financial trouble. Unfortunately the margin problem was not their only predicament. They also had a cash flow problem and they had started an internal process whereby they held back money from paying certain vendors, contractors, third parties, and even customer claims. They found out within the first month that the people in the claims department had a drawer full of customer dispute checks waiting to be sent out. Some of the checks were dated back by several months. The total of all these checks amounted to a great deal of money. Even worse than this news was the fact that even though the company was holding on to people's money, the company still had cash flow problems.

The point of all this is to encourage you to *delve into the minutia* of your company's financial picture and determine if your company is the kind of place where you want to hang your hat long term. Profits and cash flow are great predictors of a company's sustainability. Another potential land mine is a scenario where a company is highly leveraged.

HIGHLY LEVERAGED

Employees need to be on the lookout for employers that are highly leveraged. What does highly leveraged mean, and more importantly, what does it mean to you as someone looking to perhaps join such a company? A highly leveraged company is one that has an extremely high debt load. In many cases the company may not have any asset value left to borrow against due to the fact that all of the assets have already been collateralized by the lenders that made the purchase possible.

Let me give you an example of what I mean. Let's say that you have joined a company where the ownership had borrowed virtually all of the funds that were necessary for the purchase. The purchase price was $1,000,000 and the new owner borrowed the entire amount from several different lending sources. The lenders used all of the company's assets as collateral for the loan, much the same as your bank uses your home as collateral for your mortgage. These lenders will charge a much higher than market interest rate for this type of loan, and they will always be the ones to get paid first once the company is up and running. On top of the high interest rate they also took a high ownership percentage of the company in order to make sure that in the case of some unforeseen financial calamity, they would be the ones to recoup their money before any other creditors that the company may have accumulated during its course of doing business. The overwhelming amount of the initial debt load, coupled with the high interest rate and an inability to borrow any additional funds, creates a financial environment that can virtually strangle the company's potential for success. The ownership (I use that term loosely here because the lenders are really in control) is struggling from day one to keep the company afloat financially. This scenario makes for a very uncompromising situation for the ownership and for all of the employees. There is very little margin for error in this type of company. Profits are a must, revenue growth is a must, and cost containment is paramount in order to survive. You as an employee are also at risk from day one.

You may be asking why this particular ownership would take such a risk, and why the lenders would also take such a risk. In highly leveraged purchases the ownership or private equity source sees an opportunity that other people don't see. They see a company that perhaps has been mismanaged in the past. They see a company that has underutilized its assets and its market position in their industry. They see an opportunity for future success where others see a potential failure. The ownership is convinced they can turn things around, and they convince the lenders of the future potential. Then, poof, a new, leveraged buyout company is formed.

Sounds like pure magic right? Wrong, this situation is very risky and demands a lot of hard work from a lot of different players. You as an employee need to take the risk into consideration when you decide to be employed by a leveraged company, because this type of situation can mean a risk oriented sustainability assessment. In other words, will the company survive its' leveraged formation? There are a couple of other issues that you should also be looking at carefully. One is if the company is involved with other acquisitions, and another is if the company is involved with divesting portions of their asset portfolio. Both arenas can influence a company's sustainability and your own job stability.

ACQUISITIONS AND DIVESTITURES

There are times when a company expands its revenue stream by acquiring another company through an asset purchase, a stock purchase, a liquidation sale or even a merger. Acquisitions typically mean that the acquiring company has a healthy balance sheet and is in a favorable position to capitalize on the benefits that come with the acquired organization. In contrast, there are also times when a company decides to divest some of or all of its operations or assets to an acquiring company. Divestitures normally occur when a company has decided that a particular portion of its business is out of sync with their future business model and therefore becomes expendable, or when the company is in need of a cash flow infusion and does so by selling off various segments of the business. Divestitures also occur when ownership has decided to sell the business in entirety.

While this statement is somewhat of a generalization of these two business practices, I believe it is safe to say that a company is far more attractive to a new employee if it is in the acquisition mode. This usually means that the company is in an expansion mode and that might mean they are likely to add new employees to the workforce and it also might mean more stability for current employees. A company that is in a divestiture mode might mean that the company is struggling financially and therefore creates uncertainty for their employees. It clearly would be a red flag of sorts for any prospective new employees to examine carefully before making a commitment. Of course this may not hold true for a seasoned executive who has significant turnaround expertise or if you are a risk oriented individual.

Divestitures can also suggest that a company has extended itself too far over a period of time. Perhaps, as an example, they were in an aggressive acquisition mode for years, and then after a period of time the company ownership realized that their financial and management capabilities no longer matched their strategic growth objectives. So in this case the company began as an aggressive acquirer and eventually retreated into a divesting stage due to a variety of business failures. This company was an excellent employer of choice for a period of time and less than desirable choice years later. *Knowing* which stage a company is in at any given time is an important aspect of employee research and recognition.

I know of a company that for many years was adding locations around the country and even around the world. Revenues grew but additional profitability was harder to achieve. This was due to a series of issues including additional investment capital, poor management hiring decisions, a lack of geographical customer receptiveness and overall market analysis, a lack of corporate oversight, and being *too slow to recognize* all of the aforementioned impacts. Eventually the leadership was forced to either close or sell many of their market operations. This inability to correctly manage growth aspiration with growth reality caused the near downfall of the entire company. As Dirty Harry once indicated in a movie titled the same, "a man's got to know his limitations". In this particular case the ownership failed to realize their limitations both financially and managerially, which helped lead to their eventual downfall. They failed to *inspect what they expected* in a timely fashion, thereby inadvertently acquiescing field management responsibility to less than qualified people.

Acquisitions and divestitures both create sustainability issues for any company and for employees who are wondering how to best fit their future with either of these business scenarios. The above example highlights the issue of geography as another potential sustainability issue.

GEOGRAPHIC REACH

Acquisitions or other business growth opportunities that encompass an ever-enlarging geographic reach for a company may be cause for investigation before you throw your hat in the ring. The biggest issue that companies face when they start to grow geographically is people power, meaning their ability to hire and retain competent employees, and more specifically competent management personnel. It certainly is no secret that the more physical locations that a company has, the higher the difficulty with effective management of those locations.

Adding locations adds people and adding people adds layers of management and additional business complications. The entirety of the scope of operation can create all kinds of sustainability issues for a company, mainly because the ownership oversight becomes fractured, which then creates the potential for a variety of fiscal and managerial problems. There is something to say for those of you who opt to go to work for a company that has one or perhaps just a few locations, all of which are within a fairly small geographic area. The general simplicity of a business enterprise brings with it a somewhat simpler day to day operating structure. The simpler the structure the simpler it is to manage effectively, and the simpler it is for employees to engage themselves in opportunities within the company. If you like simple then as an employee you probably should be looking for employers that offer this type of culture. If you enjoy a more complex environment then perhaps you should be looking at employers that are growth oriented and geographically dispersed.

In addition to geographic reach all employees should be looking at whether the company has a succession plan in place.

SUCCESSION PLAN

Family owned businesses as well as some businesses that eventually transition to publically traded companies can do exceptionally well under the founding entrepreneur, however the future ability of that company to continue to do well depends in great part due to the ability of the entrepreneur to develop a realistic and implementable succession plan. No succession plan creates question marks for the future ability of the company to survive. Sometimes even a solid succession plan can fall to pieces and create havoc if an untimely death occurs within the family or the top managerial echelon of the company.

In my many years of working in the world of family and privately owned businesses I have seen numerous circumstances of benign neglect from company leadership when it came to solidifying the future of their organization. Why does this happen? The answer is that most of the time the rationale is as simple as ignorance on the part of leaders. Many of them make the excuse that they're too busy running the company to worry about a succession plan. Others think that they are invincible, never to walk away from the company they built and never to get gravely ill or die. They are of course deceiving themselves of reality, but trying telling them that's the case.

There are some family owned and privately held companies that are run by leaders who think they are infallible, people who believe they have all the answers and who have no use for the advice and counsel of others, especially if they're outsiders. Attempting to coax most of these people to a point of reality recognition is a waste of time, for they know all that there is to know. Be especially wary of these types of leaders because in many cases they are very likely to lead their company into an abyss of the unknowns.

Business owners in particular that think they know it all wait far too long to make a decision about what to do with their company when it comes time for them to retire. No succession plan means that they shoot from the hip and make erroneous or short sided decisions. Some will decide to sell their company, but then try to do it too late when revenues and profits are on the decline. This presents a serious issue for employees of this type of company.

Because they think know everything and listen to almost no one else, these are also the types of leaders and owners who have no clue or interest in the global environment or sustainability of the ecosystem.

SUSTAINABILITY INITIATIVES

Most of us realize today that our country and our local community, and in fact the entire world, is in some degree of jeopardy from global warming, overutilization of plastics, greenhouse gases, vehicle emissions, lack of recycling programs, unchecked deforestation, wasteful water consumption, and a myriad of other problematic ecosystem challenges. Sadly there are far too many business owners and managers who fail to take these issues seriously, and therefore they lack any inclination to implement sustainability policies and programs in their organization. Owners and top managers that espouse to saving money at the risk of further poisoning our environment and our workplaces should make you as an employee think twice before working for that kind of company.

If you find yourself working in one of these organizations you are faced with a decision of either turning a blind eye to the problem, or voicing your opinion directly to the top leadership. You can do the latter by suggesting ways by which the company can start in small ways to make changes, and doing so by spending as little money as possible. Implementing programs such as recycling paper and plastics, outright elimination of the use of plastics, converting from paper to digital, programmable utility and water use reduction, carpooling, and other similar ideas are all worthwhile objectives.

If, however, you find yourself having your ideas shot down by the leadership, and maybe even chastised for mentioning such conservation oriented plans, then I would suggest that you take a very hard look at whether this type of company is one where you want to spend the rest of your career. Companies that neglect caring for our environment may very well be equally neglectful of you and the rest of the employees when it comes to issues such as workplace health and safety. By virtue of such neglect they may also be at risk as sustainable, ongoing business concerns because of the potential of lawsuits brought about by employees, customers, vendors, the Environmental Protection Agency (EPA) or the Occupational Safety and Health Administration (OSHA).

In the next three subtitles we will take a look at a few of the internal organizational business owner or manager attitudes and outlooks that can have a significant impact on the overall sustainability of any company, regardless if it is privately or publically owned.

EXPLOITATION

I'm sure you're wondering what I mean by exploitation? A business owner or leader who makes a conscious decision to run their business by taking undue advantage of their customers, vendors or employees is engaged in exploitation. An owner or manager that continues this methodology is bound to eventually have sustainability issues.

I will again ask you to recall the company I mentioned previously whose owner wanted to serve every person in America, but only once. This particular leader had a premeditated game plan of exploiting each and every customer because the quality of service was never the foremost objective. The only objective was to sell each service component and to do by whatever means necessary, sometimes inclusive of outright fraudulent pricing and unrealistic service guarantees. That was an example of a company that intentionally exploited people for the singular purpose of financial gain.

Another example of exploitation is a company that has a hiring policy that knowingly hires people on a permanent basis but actually uses people for only a short period of time. They do this first, to hire cheap labor, and then second, to terminate employment before any benefit packages become available. This can be all too typical in companies that have an employment environment where company benefits have an eligibility time frame sixty or ninety days after the first day of employment. This scenario can happen in companies that require a lot of unskilled labor. Employee tenure is not a concern for the owners of these companies; they just need bodies so-to-speak to get manual labor needs performed as cheaply as possible.

We could also have an exploitation situation with company owners or managers who have a history of filing for bankruptcy protection. This could possibly be done to exploit vendors and contractors that are owed a great deal of money at some point in time, whereby the owner then files for bankruptcy protection to either eliminate or greatly reduce the amounts eventually paid out to the creditors. This kind of a continual business practice can be purposeful and predatory. It can also eventually damage a company's reputation and lead to an end to the business surviving at all.

The bottom line here is that you as an employee are the one that *needs to assess* your workplace environment to determine if your employer is guilty of exploitation methods, and if so, you then have the personal responsibility to either make a conscious decision to remain as an employee or to leave for a more honest and integrity oriented organization.

JAMES W. BENDER

EXPLORATION AND INNOVATION

The ideal kind of company you want to work for is one that embraces the exploration of constant operational and quality improvement methods, along with the development of new ways of doing things. The worst kind of company to work for is one where the owner or managerial leadership shoots down new ideas by saying that well, we've always done it this way and it's worked for us so far, or by simply stating that anyone with new ideas should keep them to themselves because I'm not interested. The latter kind of company may find its sustainability somewhat short lived because let's face it, *the only constant in life or business is change.* Embrace change and your company will make dust and become more prosperous. Neglect change and your company will eat dust and become a casualty of ignorance.

There are of course many companies where there is a constant goal of research and development. Companies like Apple, Google, ExxonMobil, GlaxoSmithKline and others are consistently applying the idea of exploration and improvement. Whether its technology, oil and gas, or healthcare and pharmaceuticals, the company thrives on developing the unknowns of business and life. The companies mentioned here are all publicly traded, but the main premise of creating a culture where innovation and exploration thrives as a mainstay can and should occur in every company.

While it is not a recent unknown problem (it's been going on for decades with little being done to improve things other than problem regurgitation by carriers and customers alike), the ongoing shortage of Class A truck drivers is a segment of our business culture that is now demanding real answers and solutions. It requires exploration of the unknowns and creative change to those things we do know. One idea is that drivers need to be paid more for the lifestyle they live and the service they provide. If they get paid more their employers then increase their pricing, vendors and wholesalers then increase their pricing, and finally we as end consumers bear the financial brunt of one solution to the problem. Is that a sustainable way to go about fixing this problem or in fact any problem? Solutions that are solved solely by changing wages and pricing are, in my opinion, methodologies that are not sustainable without great future sacrifices and potential calamities.

Family owned companies and private companies alike all need to be aware of change and the need for future innovation. You as an employee need to be aware of this need and take this area in consideration when making a decision about what kind of company you want to work for in the future. You will also want to be cognizant of the internal functionality of your employer.

CROSS FUNCTIONALITY

Perhaps you will recall the story I related earlier about a company I once worked for and found that the department heads weren't talking with one another or sharing important information about various policy changes they were implementing. That was an example of a *dysfunctional* workplace where everyone seemed to be oblivious to the need for sharing ideas so as not to create an unnecessary and unforeseen problem in another department.

The ideal workplace relative to functionality is one where each and every executive and each and every employee is tasked with and adheres to the credo of *unlimited information sharing*. That means no secrets are being kept, no undermining is taking place, and everyone believes that the success of the company always comes first. One of the ways to make this work in any business is to create interdepartmental teams at various levels of management. Yes, it's a bit of a force feed edict from the top down, but it's far better than the other outcome that almost always has a negative impact on the sustainability of the enterprise.

The creation of these teams will at times shine a light on certain employees who might not share the new methods. People who seek to potentially undermine the efforts of the whole are not to be trusted with additional responsibilities. In fact they are more likely to either be told to leave by company leadership, or they will make that determination on their own as they become increasingly aware that they are being exorcised from decision making participation. You as an employee will want to be aware of these types of situations and these types of potential troublemakers. You will want to steer clear of these employees to make sure that you are not tainted as being one of them by company ownership or leadership.

The issue of cross functionality in a company may also be caused in part by a management structure that is less hierarchal in nature, in other words one that has far fewer layers of management. Remember that adding layers of management creates a far more dysfunctional environment.

LESS HIERARCHY

Less hierarchy means that in most cases decisions are made easier and faster because there are far fewer layers of managerial approvals necessary for the implementation of projects. This allows for a more *functional* workplace environment and one where employee ideas and thought sharing are more apt to be embraced by ownership. This kind of environment is an ideal place for employees to flourish their careers and also where they are apt to be far happier with their leadership. It is a management structure that lends itself to a more sustainable company.

Of course no structure is perfect, so there may be times when less of a hierarchy becomes problematic. How could this possibly happen? Let's say that your company has been operating with a somewhat bloated management staff with a few too many layers. Suddenly revenues decline, profits erode, and leadership overreacts to the financial situation. The owner or manager decides one day to cut the entire first level of management, meaning those people that report directly to the top company leader. In this example we will say that this involves eight management positions, each of who had an average of ten people reporting to them. The good news from the manager's perspective is that they just saved close to a million dollars of expense. They are elated beyond belief and truly believe they have done the right thing for the company.

The bad news is that the leader now has eighty people to manage - the eight managers they had times the ten that reported to each of them. The manager soon realizes that this less hierarchal structure will not work. Managing eighty direct reports is almost impossible for anyone to handle effectively. So what does the leader do to deal with this issue? Yep, they promote eight new people to management positions and guess what? They're right back where they started, albeit they probably end up saving some amount of expense. The less hierarchal structure did not work for long.

The bottom line here is that a less hierarchal structure has a far greater use in smaller organizations where there are fewer employees. You can imagine a local florist shop that does half a million dollars in revenue with three full time employees and four part time employees. The owner of this shop can easily manage all seven of these employees. There is no need for a layer of management between the owner and the seven employees. Adding that layer would be counterproductive to the internal dynamics of the enterprise and add unnecessary expense. Less hierarchy in this case is easy and it is fundamentally sound.

Now let's take this same floral shop and say they grow twofold the following year. Now they have four full time employees and nine part time employees. What should the owner do now? What functional structure would work the best? Can the owner still manage the new group of thirteen employees with the same level of success as they could with seven employees? The answer to this question may be affected by how much work the owner does beside managing people. What if the owner is also a designer? Can they continue to take the time to design if they have thirteen employees? Does the owner want to give up the task of ordering product and supplies? Does the owner want to give up the task of being the lead salesperson? Will the owner still have time to do all the dispatching of the delivery personnel on a daily basis? Will the owner want to work seven days a week?

Wow, these are just a few of the questions this owner will need to address in order to make the appropriate decision on whether to add or name a new management position. Hierarchal decisions can have varying degrees of success in different types of situations. There is no clear cut solution or formula to adhere to. Each situation is unique and company leader needs to make the decision that best fits their individual workplace and lifestyle in order for their company to have a sustainable future. You as an employee need to be aware of these types of situations in order to best understand the internal dynamics and how they could affect you.

You will also need to pay attention to the need and quality relationship that is served by the technology capabilities of your employer, especially in a smaller company.

TECHNOLOGY CAPABILITY

Is technology a necessary evil for the sustainability of your employer? It's an interesting question based on the type of industry and the overall size and scope of how the business derives its customers. Today there seems to be an overwhelming amount of business that is derived at least partially by social media. Social media creation and implementation may require some technology expertise beyond the capability of the owner. There may also be the need for a dynamic and multifunctional website that has at its primary function the delivery of new customers. Will the owner or manager be able to handle this job without help from a technology expert?

I think it's fair to say at this juncture of business in America, as well as business around the world, technology is an absolute necessity in order to conduct almost any kind of business. That being said, the amount of external or internal technology expertise necessary will depend upon the nature of the industry, the size of the business, the growth aspirations of the owner, the financial capability of the company, and the amount of virtual customer communication requirements that are necessary for sustaining the company day by day and into the future.

Let's say that your employer owns an auto parts store, maybe even a franchise type establishment like NAPA Auto Parts as an example. You as an employee of this company will see that technology is a necessity because this is the means by which the store receives parts requests from their customers as well as the means by which they interact with their parts vendors and their corporate office. This kind of operation could potentially succeed short term without technology, but the success would most likely be short lived because of the inability to respond to customer demands in a timely fashion. Their sustainability would be at risk without the utilization of technology.

What if this type of store was more of an auto body shop? This type of shop uses an auto parts store like NAPA to fulfill its requirement for parts to properly repair their customer's cars. Let's say that in this example the auto body shop does not have sufficient technology expertise and the owner relies instead on having every single parts request and response being done via a phone call. They don't even use email to correspond because the owner is older in age and just doesn't like computers; they are more old school in their methodologies. Their invoices are hand written and receipts are done the same way (by the way, there are far more companies with owners like this than you might believe). You as a client take your car into this shop and what was promised as a one day repair turns into a three day repair by virtue of communication issues with the parts request and response. Do you think this company might have sustainability issues in the future? Even more so, what are your chances for success in this type of company?

Let's take a look now at the scenario where your employer is a local McDonald's franchisee owned restaurant. Will your employer need technology in order to sustain itself into the future? In this case your employer doesn't have the ability to say no to any new technology. Why is that? It is because the corporate office of McDonald's has realized that technology allows their restaurants to fulfill customer orders faster and more accurately by virtue of free standing kiosks instead of employees behind the counter. They can also take more orders via this method and that means more revenues for the franchisees and the company as a whole. Technology drives customer growth and brand loyalty via convenience and accuracy.

You will want to take a close look at your employer of choice to make sure that their technology capabilities are sufficient enough to sustain them into the future. You will also want to look at their ability to have written business plans and written strategic plans. Why is this important? Read on to find out.

WRITTEN BUSINESS PLAN AND STRATEGIC PLAN

Let's say that you are planning to take a trip from Baton Rouge, LA to Pocatello, ID. After much thought you make the decision to drive your car. You are trying to determine if this is the best method for your travel, both time wise and expense wise. Would you make this kind of decision without having a detailed plan?

Presumably your time frame plan would include the time it takes you to drive to the airport, park the car and take the tram to the main terminal, get through security, wait for the boarding and takeoff, air travel time, taxiway time, time to disembark, waiting time for luggage and finally the time to get to your final destination. This will build your time plan for flying, against which you will then build your time plan for driving, including stops along the way for rest, food, lodging, etc.

After building the time plan you would next build the expense plan. Your flying expense plan would include items like fuel for the car, tolls, parking fees, tips for the skycaps, airline ticket, airport food and drinks, taxi fare, rental car expenses, etc. Once you have built this plan you can then build in your driving expenses, which would include items like fuel and oil, tolls, hotels and meals along the way, and wear and tear on the car, etc.

After all of the above is done you can then make a quality decision as to whether you drive or fly, having considered both expenses and time together in order to come to your decision, which in the end is to drive the car. You put a *plan* together that verifies your decision, and which also serves as a *measurement tool* by which you can later compare your estimated times and costs with your actual time and costs. Now your written travel plan becomes something tangible, a real business plan of sorts.

Your ideal family owned employer will have a *written strategic plan and a written business plan.* What's the difference? A business plan is generally for a one year fiscal period of time. It encompasses a revenue component and an expense component, along with detailed numbers for various categories within each component. It will also include estimates for taxes, depreciation and amortization. A business plan is not just a numbers plan but also includes marketing objectives, operations objectives, personnel objectives, and a whole host of other objectives that are of importance in terms of achieving the planned numbers. It is a written plan that *enables ownership to measure the actual results* on a month to month and year to date basis against the estimated monthly and year to date objectives built into the plan. It is a plan against which the owner or manager can make timely and critical business decisions in cases where the actual results are deviating greatly from the forecasted numbers.

A strategic plan is one that provides an overall synopsis of the company's *strategic objectives over a period of years.* It could be as few as three years or it could be as many as five or ten years, but normally a strategic plan will be somewhere in the three to five year time frame. This kind of plan provides an overview of what the company hopes to achieve from a longer term business perspective. It might have some numbers attached to the plan, but if so it will only be top line oriented, perhaps more for the benefit of lenders and investors than for the ownership. It is more of a *road map to the future* than it is a day to day or month to month battle plan.

If a company is going to be sustainable into the future then it will be important to have both a written strategic plan and a written business plan. It will be up to you as an employee to determine if your employer has such plans. If so, you are at least working in an environment there is a better than average chance for success. If not, then you might be looking for a new job.

CHAPTER FIVE
SURVIVING YOUR FIRST WEEK ON THE JOB

So you finally have your job offer, and your pre-employment background and drug screenings have been successfully finalized. Hopefully you have the *offer in writing* (always ask for this) and you have read through and understand the company's employment policies and benefit package. If there are things you have read but don't understand, make a note of them so you can ask either your boss or someone in the Human Resources Department for explanations upon your arrival. It is extremely important for you to understand everything you can about your new employer's policies, processes and procedures as quickly as possible. You should do this before you show up for work, but if not then get the answers on your first day. Why is this so important?

Every company has certain guidelines that they utilize for employment practices. These cover things like their hiring process, termination process, performance expectations, sick day and vacation policies, harassment policy, dress code, and benefit package eligibility, etc. You are expected to not only know these policies but to also follow them. If you decide to not follow company guidelines then you will most likely set yourself up for failure and possible dismissal from the company. Make sure you *make it a priority* to read the policies, ask questions if you have them, and to adhere to company standards at all times. Straying from the company norms is not a good way to start things off at your new job.

Your first day and week on the job are important times for you to get acclimated to your new surroundings, but even more important for you to present yourself in the most professional manner possible. Everyone, most importantly your boss and company leadership, will be watching you with the eyes of a hawk, waiting, but certainly not hoping, for you to make some kind of rookie blunder. Focus on your *powers of observation* and learn to follow the lead of others as you make your way through the first days and weeks on the job. Your boss and higher management do not want you to screw up; after all, they made the decision to hire you. But your boss and other management will want to quickly determine if they made the right decision in hiring you. If they realize quickly that you were not the person they thought you were, they will then want to show you the exit door as quickly as possible. No company likes to carry what they refer to as dead wood for very long.

In the following subchapters we will take a closer look at the importance of being on your best behavior during your first week on the job, starting with timing.

TIMING IS EVERYTHING

Timing can be coincidental in nature or it can be preplanned in nature. Your objective as a new employee, especially in your very first week on the job, is to be timely in everything you do. On your first day you want to make sure you arrive at least fifteen to thirty minutes early; not on time, not a minute early, and certainly not late. You want to plan ahead and make allowances for traffic issues, public transportation delays, and alarm clock issues. Plan your wardrobe the night before, not the day of; plan your traffic route or your public transportation routes and timetables the night before, not the day of; plan your dinner and breakfast with the idea of not eating anything that might upset your stomach; get a good night sleep; remember the 7 "P"s - Proper Prior Planning Prevents Piss Poor Performance - *show up early!*

What other timing issues are important for you to consider during your first week on the job? How about making sure that you arrive early for any and all meetings that you are invited to attend? You will probably have a meet and greet on your first day where you are introduced to each of the other employees in the company, or if it's a large company, at least all of the employees that work in the same area or same department. Make sure you are on time for each of these meet and greets. Other employees in the company have things to do, so don't take up more of their time than is allotted on your meet and greet schedule. Be respectful of their time and be on time for every single meeting.

How about your time allotted for lunch? If you have a lunch period from 12 noon to 1 p.m. make sure you don't leave your desk or work area before noon and make sure you're back at your desk or workstation before 1 p.m. Do not abuse your lunch break time frame! Remember that your boss and maybe others too, are looking at everything you're doing on your first day and during your first week. I recall an episode years ago when a new employee went to lunch on time on their first day of employment but never came back to work at all. Now that's an extreme example of bad timing. Obviously they felt a complete disconnect to take such dramatic action, but in the end that type of timing is not what you want to follow.

Then there's the issue of bathroom breaks, smoke breaks (if you smoke at all), personal phone call breaks, etc. During your first week as a new employee you want to keep all of these issues to an absolute minimum if at all possible. I realize you have to use the facilities, just don't use the restroom as a means by which you escape your desk to make personal phone calls or waste time. Other employees will notice any undue amount of bathroom breaks and they will start to wonder, and not in a good way, what you're doing in there. Make sure you don't give anyone reason to talk about you in a potentially negative manner.

Another timing issue that I'll address here is quitting time. If you're an hourly employee and your work hours are 8 a.m. to 5 p.m., make sure you're at work and ready to do your job by 8 and still working up to 5. You do not want to be seen as someone who is a clock watcher - someone who is always looking at the time clock on the wall counting the minutes or even seconds before you can finally leave. You don't want to be seen packing up your personal belongings thirty minutes early and then standing around doing nothing.

If you're a salaried employee and the company hours of operation are 8 a.m. to 5 p.m. you again want to arrive to work early and depart your job after 5. Do not get caught in a situation where you are seen walking out the door at 4:55 p.m. or even 4:59 p.m. You are being paid to work up until and through 5 p.m. at the very least. Most salaried employees are actually expected to work beyond the normal hours of operation. Don't be seen as someone who is eager to leave the workplace, especially during your first week on the job. Play it calm, cool and collective by hanging around after the close of business hours to talk with other employees and even your boss. Be a people person by getting to know others in your department and by asking others if they need any help. Doing this will endear you to your boss and to other employees.

The last timing issue I'll talk about is one involving your delivery of requests made by your boss, the owner, or other senior level executives. As an example, if your boss or the owner sends you an email requesting an informational response of some type, don't sit on it for hours or days. It is important that you respond to emails, phone calls and face to face asks in a timely fashion. By timely I mean as quickly as you can do so with an appropriate amount of specifics as it relates to the actual request. The timeliness of your responsiveness will be something that is measured by your boss or owner, so pay attention to following up on requests made by management personnel. This is also true for any kind of written reports that you are required to submit. The bottom line is this - don't be late with anything that is asked of you, most especially during your first week of employment.

It will also be important for you to be very aware of your surroundings during your first week. This means learning to listen more and ask questions when you don't have answers.

LISTEN AND LEARN

Your first week on the job is not a time to be a know-it-all. This would be a surefire way to draw the ire your employee teammates and your boss as well. Your objective as a new employee is to be a sponge, ready and willing to absorb any and all information and insights. It's possible however that you may actually find you are the smartest person in the room so-to-speak, but this is not the time to demonstrate your intellectual prowess. Listen, observe, and learn through the words and actions of others. This methodology will help endear you to your cohorts and to your boss/owner. If you hear someone say something incorrect, don't be in such a hurry to correct them. Let someone else do that, maybe someone who has been on the job longer than your tenure of a few hours or a few days.

Let's say that your first week on the job is with a local landscaping company. Your particular job function entails learning how to operate and maintain each piece of equipment that is utilized by the company. This might include trimmers, blowers, lawn edgers, mulching mowers, riding mowers of various sizes and operational types, trenchers, augers, tillers, chain saws, spreaders, and sprayers, among others. In addition you are expected to learn how to drive, use, and maintain various types of trucks including flatbeds, utility trailers, dump trucks, and utility carts, among others. Next you are *expected to learn* how to properly use and maintain various types of tools including digging tools, cutting tools, grading tools, measuring tools and marking tools, among others.

Now I don't know about you, but to me that sounds like a lot of stuff to learn during your first week or weeks on the job. What's the best way to learn how to use all these items? You probably guessed it already - it's by listening, observing, and paying close attention to other employees who are experts at their jobs. Some of you are perhaps saying at this point that you worked with this type of equipment at your last job. You already know how to use all this equipment. Okay, maybe you did, but your new employer wants to make sure that you *do things their way, not your way.*

Remember this at all times - you are most likely not the person in charge on day one or week one. *Listen and learn.* Don't be a big shot and pretend to know everything or boss other people around.

The other thing you will want to do is ask questions, a lot of questions, not for the sake of just asking, but more so to learn things about your new job and your new employer.

JAMES W. BENDER

ASK QUESTIONS

We've already addressed the issue of asking questions if you don't fully understand your employer's personnel and employment policies. These types of questions are best addressed to your boss or the owner or the person who runs human resources. Questions that related to your particular job function should always be first addressed to your direct supervisor. You can also direct questions of this nature to other employees who have the same general type of job function, but you only do this after you ask your boss. Doing this means that you are recognizing and *adhering to the internal management chain of command*, a very important concept in virtually every company, and maybe even more so in a family owned or privately held company.

Asking questions about your job description and how best to achieve the expected results is very important for a number of reasons. As an example let's say that your first week on your new job is with a local moving company. They have hired you to be one of their helpers, otherwise known as lumpers by people in the industry. The main role is to carry furniture out of people's homes into moving trucks and then back in to their new residence as a result of their relocation. You quickly learn that there is a right way and a wrong way to carry furniture. You learn this by first observing and then asking questions of the folks that have been around for a while, the professional lumpers and professional drivers.

As a new helper you have several objectives. The first one is to never break anything. That causes a claim to be filed and your employer will not be happy with this outcome. The second objective is to perform your job in a timely fashion. If it's a local move the customer is probably paying for the services by the hour. They expect the job to be completed within a certain time frame, which means you need to hustle in order to meet the time estimate given to the customer. The third objective is to not hurt yourself or the home or your fellow lumper in the process of carrying furniture. You want to ask questions of the professionals to make sure you're doing things the right way. You will learn to lift heavy items by using your legs and not your back. You will ask questions and learn that when going up and down stairs and exiting through doorways you always move a bit slower with a bit more caution. This is to protect the furniture, the walls, the doorways, your lumper partner and yourself. You will learn how to be a good mover by asking questions, not by acting as though you know everything. This will ensure that you are retained in your job with the potential of advancement within the company.

Another area for you to ask a lot of questions is in regards to what your boss or owner expects of you from a performance perspective. If you never ask your boss what they expect of you and how they will review your work, then you will never know exactly what you're supposed to be doing and why you're doing it at all. You will want to know that your performance is being measured accurately and that both you and your owner agree upfront on the process and targets being used for the review. *Asking questions is not a sign of ignorance.* It is the means by which you will retrieve the answers that you need to be an exemplary employee.

Yet one more thing to focus on during your first week is your overall attitude; your attitude towards your boss, towards the owner or managing partner, and towards your fellow employees.

ATTITUDE MATTERS

Do you know what "swagger" means? You might see it on television during NFL football games. The 1985 Super Bowl champion Chicago Bears come to mind. The whole team had swagger; that certain look and movement and attitude that reflected the confidence that they had in their team and their teammates. They loved to showcase their stuff. They knew they were better than any other team and they wanted to show it off to the whole world. They strutted, they danced, hell they even had their own song (remember The Super Bowl Shuffle? If you're too young to remember then go You Tube it!).

Maybe you have this type of chutzpah when you show up for work on day one; you know that I've been there and done that better than anyone else type of attitude. I strongly suggest that you leave that attitude at home and that you don't act like you were part of the '85 Bears. Attitude is everything means that you want to show up with self-confidence, just not the showy, glitzy kind of self-confidence. You want to be somewhat reserved in your presentation of your persona. Don't come across with any type of sexist, racist, nationalist or pompous tendencies; just exhibit yourself as a good person with a kind heart and a good sense of humor. Do this and you will be just fine.

Having a good attitude also means showing up for work with a smile on your face every day. It means keeping that face all day long and still having that face when you leave. When people see you smiling they will have a tendency to instantly like you; to feed off your positive energy and charisma. This will endear you to other employees and to your boss or owner or manager. Staying positive is not always an easy thing to do, be it at home or while at work. Sometimes it takes a little effort to remain that way. Sometimes it takes a herculean effort to remain that way. That's what life in the trenches of work does to you from time to time. Expect it, rise up to it, and conquer it.

When you're in meetings and the owner or boss is addressing some problems with a particular issue, try not to get that look of discouragement on your face; the look that you may see on other people's faces. When times get difficult or when problems arise, you want to be the type of person who rises up with *enthusiasm and new ideas*. You don't want to be the downer type. You want to be upbeat, energetic and positive in your outlook. Believe me when I tell you that your boss, other managers, and the owner or managing partner will love you for that kind of attitude, and you will get more chances for upward job movement by exhibiting this kind of persona. During your first week on the job you will also want to be keenly aware of everything going on around you.

NOTICE EVERYTHING

You're new to the job and new to the company, so when you first show up you probably have very few ideas of what to expect. This lack of knowledge means that you might find yourself saying the wrong thing at the wrong time, or behaving badly when others are likely to notice, or staring out the window when your boss asks you a question. One of the main keys of success to your first day and first week on the job is to be super attentive; to *notice everyone, everything and every word spoken*. Notice facial expressions, gestures, and body language. Notice the way people dress and the way they say hello to the owner or manager of the company. Notice everything.

When you make the conscious decision to maximize your attentiveness during your early days, you are inherently telling yourself that nothing is going to get past you. You will see it all, hear it all and eventually know it all too. You need to act as though you're some kind of spy, not in a bad way, but in the way 007 James Bond of Her Majesty's Secret Service would notice everything and everyone around him. He did this to be aware of potential danger; to be in a position where he could respond appropriately if the need arose, and to read people and surroundings for immediate commitment to his memory. James Bond was instinctive for sure, but he learned to be that way. He learned by forcing himself to pay attention to every single detail in every single situation. That's what you need to do as well, especially during your first week on the job.

When you walk in the front door of your workplace take notice of the ambiance; the colors and photos or paintings on the walls; the floors, the work stations, the offices, and the signage that may be on the walls and doorways. Take notice of the way people are dressed. Take notice of how people move; are they striding quickly or are they walking slow? Watch if people are talking on their phones while walking, or talking with others while walking. Notice if office doors are open or if they're closed. Notice if there are clocks on the walls and if so, whether they are accurate. All of these *observations* will provide you with *clues* about your new employer, clues that will help you adjust to your new work environment, and clues that will help you to be successful. You want to make an attempt to fit in to your new surroundings and attentiveness will help you succeed.

Take special notice of how other employers interact with and speak to the owner or top manager of the company. Does the dialogue seem friendly and genuine or does it seem curt and matter of fact? Also notice how the owner or top leader responds to employees. Are they smiling while communicating or are they frowning? Is their language pleasant or is it harsh? Your powers of observation are an important attribute during your first week. Use them wisely. As an example, use the recommendations that your parents and driver education teacher gave you when you started driving. When you pull up to a railroad crossing you need to slow down or even stop; then you look, listen, look again in both directions, and then proceed with caution. In other words, notice everything going on around you. Don't take anything for granted.

Notice the boundaries that are set by the owner or manager in terms of their approachability. Notice those employees that seem to be in good graces with the owner or top leader and figure out why that might be the case. Also notice those employees that seem to be on the outside looking in as far as their relationship with the owner or manager, and again try to determine why that might be the case. You are looking for tiny hints as to the best way for you to interact with the owner and also your boss. You're trying to figure out if you have those personality characteristics that might mesh well with the company ownership. By noticing how others relate to the company leaders, you are observing how you might best handle different situations as they arise in the future. Also notice how the owner and others dress on a day to day basis.

DRESS FOR SUCCESS

Every company has some form of a dress code or policy in place. Your best option is to know that policy before your first day at work. My suggestion to you is to know the policy and then dress up from the policy standards for your first weeks on the job. Dressing up, meaning being better dressed than the policy calls for, is a way for you to display that you are serious about your role with the company. You want to convey the appearance of someone who cares about the company and also about yourself. People who take the time to care about and think about how they will look to others will have a better chance at succeeding with their employer than someone who doesn't give a hoot.

What do you think of when you see someone show up for work with rumpled clothes that appear to have just been pulled out of the hamper? What kind of impression do you get when someone shows up at the office with those kinds of jeans that have holes in them, albeit made by a designer? What are your thoughts when someone shows up without having groomed themselves in a proper manner? Sure, there are companies out there that might not have a strict dress code, but more often than not these companies are very small in size, and where the owner or upper management has a rather relaxed personal attitude towards overall appearance. These generally occur with businesses that have a rather low key approach and need to impress their client base, or where the job specifics are such that dressing up would not be such a wise choice.

I had a boss of mine years ago who was a true believer in dressing to the nines every day of the week. They would always have a formal look that mirrored the exact occasion. If there was a business meeting then it would be a finely tailored suit, a freshly pressed shirt, brightly polished wing tip shoes, a powerful red striped tie, and a color matching handkerchief precisely folded to ever so slightly stick out of the left breast-side coat pocket. Every day that I saw this person at the office they were dressed in an impeccable fashion. It became a sort of trademark look for this owner and everyone would notice and everyone would comment on the look.

When Friday came around and everyone showed up with casual wear, because that was the company policy, the owner would show up in a colorful sports jacket, crisply pressed slacks, dress shirt and tie, and the signature handkerchief hanging perfectly out of the breast pocket. They would always say that there was nothing casual about business, so dressing in a casual manner was totally foreign. I suspected then, and also now, that they never really liked people dressing in a casual manner. It just wasn't their style or comfort level. We would all do well to remember the phrase "*there's nothing casual about business*".

Take a look around at today's dress codes. Years ago when IBM decided that white dress shirts were no longer mandatory for men it changed the entire dress code landscape for office workers across the country. One by one professional companies were allowing their employees to dress in a more casual fashion, and today there are hardly any companies that require a customary suit and tie/professional dress type of look at work. In fact in lots of companies today the employees are allowed to wear jeans to the office. It's become the norm in most if not all technology oriented companies where millennials make up the primary workforce.

Dress codes in jobs where you are expected to get a bit dirty during the day have more relaxed expectation levels. Many companies in this type of work arena have dress codes that involve uniforms, in which case you as a new employee don't need to worry about what to wear to work. Your employer has already figured that out for you. Then there are jobs that are outside in nature in which case you will dress in a manner that suits the specific type of work you're going to be doing on any given day.

The bottom line that I'm trying to get across to you is this - whatever the dress code might be in your company, you are far better off dressing in a manner that *exceeds expectations*. Believe me when I say that your boss and owner will notice and it will have a positive impact on their perspective and opinion of you as a new employee. In fact you will have a far better chance of actually meeting and talking with the owner if you follow this suggestion.

MEET THE TOP BRASS

Yes, you might be a little nervous about meeting the top person in your company, but that's only natural. But let me key you in on a little secret - most people are more nervous than you think you are, and most employees will not build up the nerve or create an opportunity to meet the top brass. What's the advantage of meeting the top leaders you might ask, especially if you're starting out at a relatively low level job? Let's say that you've just started working at a local grocery store, and let's say that store is Aldi's. Perhaps you don't recognize that name, so let me give you a few details before I answer your query.

Aldi's is a boutique grocery store chain that was founded in Germany during the 1960's by the Albrecht family. They have stores in over 20 countries and now have almost 2,000 store locations just in the U.S. Today they employ over 25,000 people and the company continues its history of expansion and renewal. They have a very loyal customer base that enjoys the company mantra of providing quality products at reduced prices in a no frills shopping environment. So yes, your new job might be as a lower level employee to start, but with the size and number of locations that the company has, I would suggest to you that your prospects for future advancement are pretty solid if you're a go-getter type of employee.

Here's how I would suggest that you handle your first day, week and month on the job - get to work early, wear the uniform they provide with pride and keep it clean, ask questions if you're not sure of something, work hard and be nice to people that you work with and to customers, stay on the job later if they allow you to do so, and try to meet the general manager of your store as quickly as possible. After you meet the store manager then figure out how to meet the area manager and then the regional manager and then any higher level manager that happens to visit your store. You do all of this just be being present and saying hello to these executives with a big smile on your face. You will get noticed if you make the attempt to get noticed, not be being a wall flower hiding in the bathroom or in a warehouse closet.

Meeting the owner or top executive of the entire company might be difficult in this size company, but you may very well get that opportunity if you follow the path that I just laid out for you above. Getting ahead in this type of company requires you to meld well with both store staff and store management, and by letting managers at every level know that you are willing to work hard by accepting promotions and relocations if and when opportunities are presented. Meet as many management people that you can and focus on making the best *first impression* each and every time you have that kind of opportunity. The next few subtitles will focus on tips that that you can follow in order to make that best first impression.

SOCIAL MEDIA IS NOT YOUR FRIEND

I guess that these days most everyone is on some kind of social media platform, both searching for and sharing various tidbits of information with personal connections as well as connections of friends. You might be inclined to get home after your first day or week on the job and share the highlights or lowlights of your employer or your boss or your fellow employees. This is something that you do not; I say do not want to do. The last thing you want to do is to have the owner or your boss find information posted about their company or worse yet about them personally, and have it traced back to you as the originator of the posts. If this happens and you are the culprit so-to-speak, then you may very well have to be looking for new employment rather quickly.

Social media is not your friend when it comes to your job. If you feel the need to share personal information do so with information that is not job related, most especially during your early days and weeks on a new job. Remember that your employer will be watching you very closely and looking for any reason that might give them cause for alarm or thoughts that they may have made a mistake by hiring you. Make a pledge to yourself that your employer and your fellow employees are off limits from a social media perspective during your first week or weeks.

Another word of caution is this one - using social media during work hours is a big no-no. You are being paid to work not to be a social media wizard. Maybe it's okay to do a little of this during your work breaks, but never during work hours. I've had employees do this in the past and I found out about it because other employees in the office would bring it my attention - how did they know you're asking? Well, because they too were on social media during the same time. How's that for the pot calling the kettle black! I also found out about it from people outside the company who just happened to be on social media when my employee was surfing. You might imagine my frustration with this kind of employee; wasting time and getting paid for it.

YOUR CELL PHONE IS NOT YOUR FRIEND

As social media is not your friend, your cell phone is also not your friend, especially during your first week or weeks on the job. Obviously if you are making the mistake of using social media, then you are most likely doing so via your cell phone. Geez, how many mistakes can you make at the same time? Here is the best way to handle your cell phone during work hours - put it on airplane mode or just turn it off completely. You can always check your phone during break times to make sure you have not missed any really important family type calls. Your personal cell phone should never be ON, meaning you can hear the ring or the buzzing, during work hours. Again, you are being paid to perform some type of work, not to talk on your personal cell phone or to be surfing on social media or to be playing video games.

In the next chapter we will be preparing you on how to be on the lookout for certain types of fellow employees who may not have your best interests at heart.

CHAPTER SIX
SURVIVING YOUR PEERS (BEWARE)

Regardless of what kind of company you go to work for you will undoubtedly work in an environment where there are other employees present. One of them might be your boss; unless it's the owner or company CEO directly (we will not characterize the owner as an employee in this section). Others might be your peers; employees that have the same basic status on the organization chart that you do. Still others might be employees who work in job positions that are below your level on the organization chart, and there will also be employees who rank above your status but are not your direct supervisor. Every single one of these employees can have an impact on your success with the company, some more than others, especially your peer group.

Your peer group will almost always be comprised of people who have the same objective that you do - to work hard, be successful and get promoted to career changing opportunities. Therein lays the peer group pressures and complications. Everyone wants the same things that you do, which means you and they are in a competition for a promotion and to be noticed by the boss or owner or top leader. Some of your peers will be great people to work with and who will never try to undermine your very existence at the company. Others however will not be so kind, and they may very well do everything in their power to oust you from the company by whatever means necessary. Remember the note I mentioned earlier in the book about making dust or eating dust? The latter group of peers will want to make you eat as much dust as they can muster up, and they will use a variety of dirty tricks to take advantage of you. *Beware* these people; beware their underhandedness; beware the wolf in sheep's clothing.

THE MANIPULATOR

These are your peers who are trying to get you to do something that they don't want to do themselves. These are the people who are trying to get you to do something they know will turn out badly. These are the people who will sweet talk you up one side and down the other, but all along their objectives are to convince you to do something that will most likely make you look bad to the boss or owner so that they will end up looking better by your demise in stature.

No doubt some of you can recall times gone by when one of your siblings manipulated you and somehow got you in trouble with your parents. Or maybe you yourself manipulated your parents in some way shape or form to get something that you wanted. Most likely we've all experienced some form of being manipulated or being the manipulator at some point in time during our past, especially as children. Hopefully most of these childhood manipulations ended without too much harm being done to anyone involved, and hopefully they were forgotten and forgiven by the participants. Engaging in manipulative tactics in the workplace, however, is a far different and more serious offense.

I've seen far too many instances of underhanded manipulation during my years as an employee and as an employer. I can recall one situation where an employee who was working on a specific project with a couple of team members came up with three options for solving the particular problem at hand. This employee was supposed to take the three options to their boss and a committee assigned to address this project, wherein the group as a whole would review the pros and cons of each option. Instead of following the proper channels of internal communication, this employee decided to solicit the "help" of the newest colleague, with the idea of manipulating this colleague into taking the worst of the three options and writing up a detailed recommendation to the committee. The colleague was unaware of the fact that they had been manipulated into thinking they had the perfect solution, and in the end they were thoroughly embarrassed by the presentation to the committee.

I can recall another episode of manipulation by a boss of mine years ago when I had a management issue of serious consequence on my hands. A direct report of mine was accused by several staff members in the office of sexual harassment and preferential treatment. According to the overall company human resources manual it was clearly a situation that was designed to be dealt with by only the most senior management personnel in the company. In this particular case the person designated to handle this apparent transgression was my direct superior. While I won't go into any specific details, my boss decided to use their inherent hierarchal authority to insist that it was indeed my responsibility to deal with this problem. I was in effect manipulated into dealing with a serious human resources infraction that should have been dealt with by someone in a higher position, someone who did not have the alleged perpetrator as a direct report.

JAMES W. BENDER

THE LIAR

These are your peers who will just flat out lie to your face in order to make you look bad or to strengthen their own agendas. They might tell you that an important meeting starts at 10 a.m. when in fact it starts at 9 a.m. You end up waltzing in at 10 when the meeting is starting to break up, and the boss or owner looks at you with a quizzical expression as if to say, where the hell have you been? The rest of the staff looks at you with smirks on their faces, knowing full well that you've been snookered. You become water cooler fodder for the remainder of the day. Not good for sure. What was the answer to this issue? The answer is to never take anyone's word for a meeting start time. When in doubt check with the person who called the meeting or better yet check your email calendar one more time. Relying on your peers for help is something you put on the back burner.

Another type of liar is the one who doesn't lie directly to you, but does so to the owner. This person spreads lies about you to your boss and to other employees, such that you are blindsided by the events. You are caught off guard by the flow of misinformation that you were completely unaware of at the time of the lies. This kind of peer will rat on you. This kind of peer will do anything they can to make you look bad. This kind of peer may look like your friend but in reality they may very well be your archenemy. They will make sup stories about you, maybe even lie to people about personal issues in addition to business issues.

So what you do when you come across someone who lies to your face and lies to your boss and lies to other employees? The first thing you do is make sure you have *all the facts* about who said what to whom and at what time and at what place. You do not want to have a confrontation or meeting with anyone unless and until you have the facts about what was said. Once you do have the facts, you will then ask for a one on one meeting with someone in human resources or the owner, during which you will call their attention to the facts as they are. By doing this you have confronted the troublemaker head on and made sure that the owner is aware of the situation. Afterwards you will do everything possible to avoid the liar in question.

I once had a salesperson leave the company for non-performance reasons, and I specifically remember telling them that they needed to leave behind all of the sales materials, files and customer notes prior to departure. The employee said they would do so. Thirty minutes after they left I found out that the files and customer notes were gone. The sales rep had lied to me; lied to my face and actually broke the employment agreement that they willingly signed when they first became an employee of the company. I had to call this person on their cell phone and tell them that I was calling the police and reporting the documents as stolen. I told them they had fifteen minutes to return all of the documents or the police would be looking to arrest them in short order. What did I learn from this experience? Never again did I allow someone who left as an employee to do so without me first checking their desk and file cabinets to ensure that everything was being left intact. I was lied to once and got taken advantage of, but I never got lied to again for that same circumstance. You always have to be wary of liars because some of them are habitual liars. Be very careful to keep these folks as far away from you as possible.

THE KISS ASS

You can already guess who this person might be in your peer group. They are the one who tells the boss or owner whatever might ingratiate them for preferential treatment. They are the people who will fawn all over the owner or manager, inflating their ego at every opportunity with flattering remarks. They might say some over the top things about the owner's appearance or their intellectual prowess or their ability to manage people or how right they are all the time. These are your peers who try to make themselves look better in the boss's eyes by lavishing praise on them, by kissing their ass as often as possible. Sure, most of them are disingenuous most of the time, but sometimes their actions and words actually work. Sometimes the owner or boss will fall for this line of bullshit; perhaps because they're new to management or perhaps because their ego needs some stroking and they enjoy the accolades. Regardless of circumstance the kiss ass peer can be a thorn in your side if you're not careful to notice who they are and how they go about their ass kissing.

The kiss ass may also try to spend some after work time with the boss or owner. This might entail cocktails after work, lunch or dinner engagements, and perhaps even an attempt at creating a personal relationship. This kind of activity goes well beyond the normal meaning of a kiss ass, but nevertheless this activity can at times have a positive outcome for the kiss ass. You will need to be very aware of this type of peer, as their efforts are generally done to serve their own personal interests at the expense of the interests of other employees, including you perhaps.

How do deal with this kind of situation when you see it happening? Your best bet is to get noticed by your boss or the owner of your employer by exceling at your job. In my experience as an employee and as an employer, there is no question in my mind that what means the most to me is how well you perform in your job. I never was one who cared for employees trying to ingratiate themselves to me, but that's just me. I'm certain that there are managers and owners who do like the extra attention from employees. I would just say that in the end your performance on the job will be the most important thing that propels you toward better positions and improved compensation opportunities.

One other thing you might also want to do is take some time to get to know your boss or owner on a more professional basis. Does this mean spending time after working hours? No, it does not. It means asking questions of the right nature at the right time. If you're in a meeting with the owner or top manager that's the time to probe for details on how the business was started, objectives for the future of the business, and other similar queries that are professional in nature, not personal in nature. Keeping your relationship on a professional basis is always the right decision to make, especially as a new employee looking to make a judicious impact. This methodology is significantly more professional that being a kiss ass, the latter of which will, more often than not, get you into more trouble than it's worth.

THE WOLF IN SHEEP'S CLOTHING

I'm going to go out on a limb here and hope that most of you have heard about a Disney movie titled *The Three Little Pigs*. Or perhaps you've heard the story about a fox guarding the hen house? If not, no worries because I'm going to explain things to you right now.

The gist of The Three Little Pigs story revolves around a wolf that desperately wants to get at three little pigs for a nice meal. Of course the three pigs live inside a house and they all know what the wolf looks like and why the wolf is so anxious to get at them. The wolf is constantly frustrated by the inability to figure out how to get the three little pigs out in the open. In the end the wolf decides to dress up in sheep's clothing as a disguise so that the pigs will allow the wolf to come inside their house. The moral of the story is that you always need to be aware of the fact that what you see, or perceive as seen to be real, might very well be something completely different.

The story about the fox and the hen house is similar in nature. Knowing full well that a fox would thoroughly enjoy finding and killing hens for a meal, you would therefore surmise that you would never allow a fox to guard a hen house, right? There is an inherent conflict of interest in putting a fox in charge of guarding a hen house. The fox might tell you that all will be well and that the hens will be just fine with the fox in charge, but in reality you would know deep down that what the fox said was complete bullshit. The business side of this story is that you always want to make sure that you are wary of bad intentions coming across as the best of intentions.

In business settings the wolf in sheep's clothing might very well be one of your peers who comes across as someone who really likes you; someone who really wants you to be their friend; someone who really wants to help you succeed at your job; someone who is endearing and who goes out of their way to do things for you. The problem with all of this behavior is the possibility that your peer is setting you up for some kind of failure, or setting you up to take the blame, or setting you up to take undue advantage of you and the work you do. This kind of peer is like the wolf, not because of what they wear, but because of their efforts to deceive you into thinking that that they are there to help you at every turn and every opportunity.

So the real question is this - how do you spot the wolf in sheep's clothing? You show up for work at your company and you meet a few, or maybe fifty, or maybe even hundreds of fellow employees. You work side by side with these people, some of whom are your peers, meaning those employees who share the same position as you on the overall organization chart. You believe, or at least hope, that the vast majority of your peers are good people. So how do you spot the bad actors? What signs are you looking for in identifying the wolf?

First, the wolf will be overly flattering to you directly and about you to others. They start this way because they're setting the stage for later. Second, the wolf will look for ways to endear their goodness on your behalf. They will do unsolicited favors for you. They will jump in and help you with work projects or ask if they can do some of your work for you. Again they are setting the stage for later. Third, the wolf will look for an opening in your armor. Your armor includes the sensory perceptions that you have as a person to guard against people who might be looking to take advantage of you. The wolf is looking for your weaknesses. Maybe you're too nice. Maybe you believe everything people tell you. Maybe you are afraid of confrontational situations. Maybe you have a history of looking the other way when you see something that's wrong. The wolf will look to take advantage of whatever weaknesses they can find, and then they will act on those weaknesses. They will act as though they were your friend, only to turn on you when the time is ripe for them to do so in order to take advantage of a particular situation.

The bottom line is this - study people's habits and look for things that seem out of the norm or out of character for the typical person you know. If you see or sense something out of the ordinary take appropriate action to guard your well-being from a would-be wolf. Distance yourself from this kind of person, and do it quickly. Another kind or peer to stay away from is the leech.

THE LEECH

You probably know what a leech is right? It's a blood sucker - a predatory worm with suckers at both ends that latches on to your body to suck the blood out of you. You can't pull it off of you because the mouth part might remain under your skin. You have to burn it off or use alcohol or table salt to remove it. In other words this creature loves to get under your skin and stay there to suck your blood as long as they can.

In business this kind of person is one who might extort profit from you or at the very least sponge off your efforts. This kind of person will wait until you've finished a project or a task and then do their best to take credit for everything you've worked on. They will also look over your shoulder to do their best to find out what you're up to in order to find a way to accomplish your task or assignment before you do. They will look for any way possible to take advantage of you for as long as they can.

When we were younger and still in school we all used to be wary of the classmate that did their best to sneak a peek at our homework or test answers. We most likely called this person a cheater, but they also acted as a leech looking to take full advantage in any way they could to steal our work. We somehow knew who these kids were and would be careful to hide our answers during tests in class. Sometimes however, these leeches would also be bullies, and they would use their bully status to threaten some of us into doing things that we knew were wrong, and where we might actually get caught and get in trouble with the teacher. The leech is the type of person who relishes taking advantage of you, while simultaneously seeing you getting snared in some kind of dishonest scheme or plot. What did you do at the time when this happened back in school? Maybe you asked your teacher to change your seating assignment in class to make sure that the leech was never close enough to you proximity wise to take advantage of you. Or, maybe you never did anything, and allowed yourself to be a victim of the leech.

In your work environment you always want to be on the lookout for the leech. Trust me when I say that they exist in every workplace. You may not see them or notice them right away, but they are there, ready to pounce on any opportunity that you might unknowingly give them.

How will you know who they are? You might notice one of your peers being a bit too chummy with you and always inquiring about what you're working on or how you handle a certain task or project. They might come across as genuinely sincere in the thoughts while secretly trying to gain the knowledge that you possess for their own benefit. They stand too close to you or sit too close to you in meetings. Why would they do this? Because they want to hear everything you say or that others say to you. They want see what you're doing. They want to be a sponge and soak up as much of your knowledge and efforts as possible.

Recognize the leech for what they are. They are looking to live off of your own personal work and accomplishments. They are looking to succeed by getting as close to you as possible so that they might be able to *sponge off your efforts*. They want to be your friend because they think that you might be naïve enough to continue to drag them with you everywhere you go and with everything you do. Figure out who they are and stay away from them, as far away as possible.

THE BOSS'S KIDS

Let's use this scenario as an example of what I mean here. You start working for your company and quickly find out that the boss's oldest kid, or maybe even the youngest kid, is one of your peers. The boss wants the kid to work in the trenches just like you, presumably in order for the kid to learn various jobs by actually doing that kind of work. Generally this is a good move by the owner or partner in charge in terms of making sure the kid understands the business from the bottom up. However, this can also be a dicey scenario for you. Why you might ask? It's because this kid who is now your peer, might eventually be your boss. That's the way some family owned companies work, and even some privately held and publically traded companies. Family members have an edge in reaching the top echelon of the company; worker bees like you do not have the family connection.

So how do you deal with this issue of working side by side as peers with the owner's oldest or youngest kid? Do you have an objective to be their friend? Is your objective to stay as far away from this kid as possible? Here's some advice for you - be on your best behavior at all times because you never know what the kid is going to tell the owner about who and what you are. The kid can be a buddy or the kid can be a tattletale. You really don't want to do anything to find out which one they are. As the oldest kid this person is likely next in line to take over the reins of the company once the owner/founder/partner decides to retire. If you like the company and your job, then you want to make sure that this kid has the highest opinion possible of your work and your work ethic.

You run a serious risk if you decide to befriend this kid and maybe start to socialize with them. This kind of fraternization activity may seem to be helpful for you at first, but mark my word; the day will come when your version of friendship gets tested. You will learn that in a family friendly company, family always comes first, regardless of what kind of relationship you think you might have with the oldest or youngest kid. The family is rarely at risk, but you are always at risk.

Another suggestion - don't get caught trying to date one of the boss's kids and don't be tempted to respond to an overture from one of the kids about going out on a date together. Dating the boss's kid is never a good idea, regardless of what you might see on television or in movies or read in books. Sure, you might read about someone eventually marrying into the boss's family this way, but those kinds of end results happen very, very rarely. In most circumstances when this type of dating situation occurs, the end result is you end up being a liability to the kid, and when that happens your walking papers are almost guaranteed.

THOSE WITH TENURED SERVITUDE

These are members of your peer group who have been with your employer for quite some number of years. In other words they have tenure with the organization. But there is something to be aware of in this kind of situation. Sometimes an employee with tenure has a tendency to use their tenure as a hammer over your head. What do I mean by that? This kind of peer likes to flaunt their tenure to get their own way with other employees who have far less tenure. They like to think that their tenure means that they know more than you do, and that their employment is much more secure than yours. They use this to intimidate you and to make you feel like an inferior employee to them.

This kind of peer is one that will come across as bossy and with a superiority complex, especially over newer employees who may not have the confidence to speak up among their more tenured peers. Also, these peer types are usually older people due to the tenure issue. You will have to be careful with how you handle this kind of peer. You can learn from these tenured peers but you can also get bogged down in old and traditional ways of doing things. They will always want to do things their way because that's the way they're been doing things for years. You will want to listen and learn, but to also carefully contemplate everything they say in order to avoid falling victim to possible archaic methodologies and processes.

Tenured peers will try to take center stage at every possible moment. Why do they do this? They want notoriety for sure, but they also want and need to re-establish their identity within the organization. They achieve this by always being the first person to respond to any programs that require volunteers. They know and understand how the organizational structure operates, and they find ways to consistently put themselves in the forefront as often as possible. By doing this they simultaneously put you as a newer employee in a situation where your name and your involvement in day to day work go unnoticed by your superiors.

When you find yourself in this kind of situation you can either submit yourself into a position of inferiority, or you can do your best to break the bond of tenured servitude employees by ignoring their self-made rules and protocols. Your career depends more on how you perform than on how you interact with the tenured souls who feel superior just because they've been with the company for a longer period of time.

THE UNDERMINING BULLSHIT ARTIST

I'm sure you already know people that fit this description. These are your members of your peer group that have the uncanny ability to sound smart while spewing pure bullshit. They will tell you one thing while meaning something entirely different. They will tell you about some due date for a project to be completed but it will be a date that is a week past the actual due date. These bullshit artists are not your allies. Their goal is to undermine you whenever they get the opportunity to do so. Why would they do this you might ask?

By undermining your opinions or your perspectives or even your existence, this kind of peer hopes to gain an edge with the boss and/or the owner. Any amount of negativity that the undermining bullshit artist can lay at your doorstep can give them increased leverage and notoriety within the organization. If they can make you look bad or look foolish or make bad decisions, they can then lay claim to making them look better and more important and more valuable. Let's say as an example that one of your peers tells you that they overheard the owner describing a soon to come reorganization of the department that you work in. They tell you that both your jobs may be in jeopardy. This news gets you to thinking, perhaps more than you should, because you don't want to believe it. You tell your peer in confidence that you're going to start looking for a new job. Your peer is elated, because that's exactly what they wanted all along; to push you out of the company so that they would become more important and more necessary. You find a new job within a short period of time, but it's not exactly what you wanted. You resign from the company and the owner calls you into the office and asks why you're leaving. You say that you were concerned about losing your job when the reorganization takes place. The owner or manager looks at you quizzically and tells you that they have no idea what you're talking about. You are dumbfounded and confused, and suddenly you realize that you have been lied to and undermined by your peer. You have been had; you believed someone you should not have believed. You did not verify the information they imparted on you. You have been the victim of a bullshit artist.

The moral of the story here is to be careful of peers who appear to be overly helpful with your career. They may be sincere, but they may not be sincere. You need to be constantly *aware of your surroundings* and what your peers say to you. I don't want to say that you can't believe anything that anyone says to you, but I can say that you need to be wary of everyone and make informed decisions at all times. Ask questions and think things through before you react to what someone tells you.

THE SPY

Let me warn you now - the spy is a plant. No, this is not the kind of plant that you see in a greenhouse or in a garden nursery. This is the kind of plant you really need to be concerned about at all times. This kind of peer has the ear of the boss or the owner. They will take everything they see and hear to the boss. If you say something or do something wrong, it will come as no surprise that the owner or manager will hear about it from the spy.

The spy may be someone who is actually planted in your midst by the owner. This is done in a premeditated fashion because the owner or manager wants to know everything that goes on in their company. This usually happens with owners and managers who are insecure about their employees and probably about just about everything. They have a lack of trust that is inherent in their persona, and spying on people is the way in which they ensure that they are not taken advantage of by anyone else.

The other kind of spy is the one that is self-appointed. This is the peer who decides on their own to be a spy, because this is the way by which they will gain favorable access to the owner or top company leader. When they hear something that they think the owner or leader will not approve of, they will take that information to the owner and share all the details of who, what, when, where and why. If the leader is someone who trusts no one, then the peer will be welcomed with open arms. If the owner is the trusting type, then the peer may very well have put themselves in a less than favorable light.

You will usually find out if you have a spy in the midst if you begin to hear gossip going on in your work environment. Another way you might find out is if you find that the manager is taking exception to another one of your peers. This will come about after the spy shares some unflattering information about a peer, and the owner is seen taking that peer to task in some form. If you encounter a spy then you need to be exceptionally careful with what you say to this person. Better yet, you should try your best to say nothing to this person at all. That is probably not possible if you and the spy are in the same department, but regardless of how close your work relationship might be proximity wise, you will do yourself a favor by finding ways to distance yourself from this type of person.

In the next chapter we will take a look at how to best survive your boss at work. There are all kinds and types of bosses, and hopefully the ones you will have over the course of your career will be kind, nurturing and honest. Unfortunately there may very well be a few along the way that do not fit that mold. This next chapter will highlight a number of characteristics of bosses that are not so flattering, and we will delve into how to detect who and what they are, and better yet how to deal with them in the best manner.

CHAPTER SEVEN
SURVIVING YOUR BOSS

I think we would all agree that our boss, regardless of where we work, is an important person in our working life. This person can be responsible for hiring you, for cultivating the best out of you, for promoting you, for firing you, for recommending raises for you, and for a good portion of your overall happiness on the job. In other words, your boss has a great deal of influence on your daily work life for sure, but also your overall sense of happiness and contentment with your life in general.

For all you men reading this, remember the phrase "happy wife, happy life"? This phrase means that if you try your best to keep your wife happy, then most likely you will be happy as well. In contrast, if your wife is unhappy then you are likely to be unhappy. While this phrase is somewhat sexist in nature and description, the point of the phrase overall is that certain events in one's life have an impact on other aspects of one's life. This same ideology holds true for everyone's work life and personal life balance. If you're unhappy at work then you are probably unhappy at home as well. People who are unhappy with their company, their actual position within a company, their boss, their pay check, or a host of other work related issues are very likely to bring that unhappiness home with them every day. When you bring the baggage at work home with you, then you are likely to harness that baggage throughout your personal life. *Life is a series of interactive events.*

There are all kinds and types of bosses in the world of business, and there are all kinds of descriptive phrases that pinpoint their variances from one another. As an example, there are short bosses, tall bosses, skinny bosses and overweight bosses. There are bosses with glasses, bosses with contacts and bosses that have no need for either. There are male bosses and female bosses. There are bosses of all races and creeds. There are nice bosses and not so nice bosses. There are bosses that know what they're doing and bosses that don't have a clue. There are bosses that care about you and there are bosses that care only about themselves. The point here is that bosses are each different from one another in some way, shape or form, and you as an employee will want to be aware of what type of boss that you have in your role with your employer.

This chapter outlines several different kinds of bosses, mostly the ones that you will hopefully not have as your direct boss. These are the ones that you will need to be especially wary of as you march through your career. These are the ones that could derail your career or worse. These will be the ones that you will want to avoid if at all possible. In any case you will want to figure out who and what you have as a boss as fast as you can in order to minimize any potential damage to your own career. *Figure things out fast* and you have a better chance of knowing how to deal with the situation that you find yourself in.

There are plenty of wonderful bosses in the world, far more good ones that not so good ones. Nevertheless the bad ones are out there, and my goal here is to help you assess and determine which ones to shy away from if you have the opportunity.

JAMES W. BENDER

THE NARCISSIST

We all know someone (probably more than just one), who exhibits the characteristics of a narcissist. It may be someone you know at work or it may very well be someone in your personal life. This person is difficult enough to deal with in your personal life much less your working life. In your personal life you can easily cut this person out of your life, unless of course the person is a close family member. Then you have a different set of issues to deal with, especially at family functions.

Dealing with a narcissistic boss, however, is a much more challenging scenario to cope with on a day to day basis. The narcissist is almost unbearable to be around. They lack empathy, which means if you have some kind of personal issue that requires you to take some time off, the narcissist will throw their arms up as if to say "and how does that affect me?" They have no comprehension of your problem and they frankly don't care. They are focused singularly on their own issues at hand.

The narcissist is a boss who revels in their own state of self-importance and is always geared up for additional praise, attention and adoration from everyone around them. Show them some love (not in a romantic or sexual sense) and they might become a nicer person to you, although there is no guarantee that will occur. The narcissist is also someone who has a sense of unabridged entitlement, meaning that they can do or take just about anything they want at any time they want from anyone they want. They are selfish as all hell.

This kind of boss is abnormally suspicious and envious of people who work for them, and of their peers, and even of their own boss. They seem to think that everyone is out to get them, and therefore they guard their own sense of territory with a distrust of everyone around them. Gaining their trust is virtually impossible.

Lastly, the narcissist is as arrogant a person as you will ever meet, and on top of that characteristic is the fact that they will be supremely judgmental of everything and everyone around them. Remember that they are selfish and self-important, so the arrogant and judgmental aspects of their personality should come as no surprise to anyone.

Unfortunately if you find yourself working for someone like this you may find it difficult to gain any respectful conversation or helpful advice. Given that they distrust just about everyone, they think that helping others will inevitably lead to their own downfall. The narcissist will be right and you will be wrong. If you do come up with a great idea, it will soon be their idea. If you are a salaried employee, be prepared to work after hours with nary a mention of how it impacts your personal life. Remember, they lack empathy.

So what do you do with one of these egomaniacs? First, they are not likely to change their stripes and all of a sudden become someone different. Second, you will not likely get the praise or respect that you deserve, so don't look for that to happen. Expect to be treated poorly the vast majority of the time. Third, look for avenues of escape as soon as possible without creating more of a toxic environment than already exists. You don't want to be caught in more of a no-win situation than you are already in. Fourth, if you make the decision to complain about your narcissistic boss to people higher up the ladder, don't expect anything good to come from it. You may get heard, but everything you say will likely get back to your boss. Fifth, if you follow through with number four above, your boss will not be prone to forget your insubordination (as they see it). Your life at work may become worse than it was previously. You may have to look for a new role in the company or a new job altogether.

JAMES W. BENDER

WIN AT ALL COSTS

The boss that seeks to win at all costs is a lot like the narcissist. Morals and honesty mean very little to this person. Winning means everything all the time. This might be the kind of person who can't stand losing at anything, including board games, ping pong, darts, or any other type of game or situation that has an end game winner and loser. They are very competitive in all aspects of their life, and cheating is not beyond them as they seek to put a big "W" on their personal scoreboard. Winning in a business environment might include bait and switch tactics, exaggerating facts to clients and employees, lying to employees in order to get them to do something that will help achieve success, blaming you and your work for any kind of failure, and terminating your employment with a streak of vicious slander and disrespect.

How will you know that you've got this kind of boss? You will notice that your boss will get easily agitated when things don't go as planned. There may be some yelling and screaming, sometimes at you and/or others, and sometimes just randomly at no one in particular. Loss of temper is an early sign of someone who hates to lose. They will look for someone to blame, and that could mean you, in which case you may find yourself being walked out the door.

Another sign is when your boss asks you to fudge a number or some other statistic on a report for upper management or for a customer. Maybe the real numbers don't look so good, so your boss will take the liberty to embellish a bit. The real sticking point here is if you are the one that is asked and tasked with changing the numbers or the verbiage. If you do it then your boss can deny that it was their idea. You will be the one blamed for an errors or omissions that occur. You see, the boss likes to win, so if there's any chance of losing/getting caught, they want to make sure they make someone else the fall guy, so-to-speak.

I've known people that fit this description, and all I will say is that they usually end up getting caught with some travesty, but you don't want to be the one that is left holding the bag while your boss sits back with a grin on their face. Yes, they usually get found out, but more often than not, it's too late. In the meantime there could be a history of carnage (not literally) that can be traced back to this kind of boss or owner. In general you want to remain as far away as possible from yellers and screamers. They are generally tyrants with little empathy.

WIN AT YOUR EXPENSE

This boss or owner wants to win at any expense, but mainly yours. They want to use you and your expertise to gain success. Let's take a look at a few examples of what I mean here.

Example number one has you as a new front counter order taker at a fast food restaurant. Your interview is with the owner of the franchise, and you learn during the interview that the store you have been hired at has had a tough time creating a customer foothold in the community. You are well known in the community by virtue of being on a variety of athletic teams in high school and your parents are active in community politics and nonprofit organizations. Your owner is hoping that your connections will bring new customers to the store and in fact during your first month on the job, sales skyrocket to new all-time daily highs. You have been an employee for two months now and things are going even better than the owner expected, which is why you are shocked one Friday afternoon to learn that your job is being eliminated. Your owner tells you that they are reducing headcount and since you are the employee with the least amount of tenure, you are being laid off. How does this scenario make you feel? Do you feel used? Do you feel cheapened by the string of events? Do you think you were used? You are probably replying yes here, and now recognize that your owner has won at your expense. You were indeed used as a means to drum up new business, and it worked.

Example number two involves you as a star salesperson who the owner hired away from the competition. The owner knows that you know a lot of the customers that they don't have yet. You are given your target list and marching orders as to who to call on first for new business. Within the first several months you find that you are scoring some nice wins. New business starts coming in the door. All the while you notice that the new customers are all given contracts as part of the sales process. You also notice that none of the contracts have your name anywhere on the paperwork. The only names on the contract are the company name and the owner's or manager's name, because the authority figure is the only one that had the legal authority to sign the documents on behalf of the company. It's month six and things are going well, you think, until one day you are terminated. No reason is given other than the company needs to reduce expenses. Do you feel that you have been cheated and lied to? Do you feel that you were taken advantage of by the owner or manager? Do you think you are a victim of your owner or manager winning at your expense?

These are just two examples of how owners and managers can take advantage of new employees. There are many other examples that I could list but I think you get the idea here. The answer to solving the above examples deals with being very specific about job functions and accountability when you are first interviewed. After you get the specifics nailed down, you then want everything put in written form in order to avoid complications down the road. Owners and other leaders may try to take advantage of you by not putting anything in writing. If you find that this is the case, then I would suggest that you think about looking in a different direction for employment.

THE HARASSER

There is nothing worse than finding out that you are working for a harasser, especially if you are a female. You may not detect this issue right away, but eventually you may notice that your boss is staring at you far too often and for far too long a period of time. Your boss may start to make suggestive remarks about your appearance. Your boss may start to make further remarks that are sexual in nature, going so far as to intimate that that the two of you should spend some time together after work. Perhaps the after work discussion revolves around having drinks together and then heading to a nearby motel.

The harasser is someone who generally won't stop the harassing, even if you ask them to do so. This is a pattern of behavior that they have become used to, and they find it entertaining and empowering. Someone who is a harasser gets a feeling or surge of power when they engage in harassing an employee. The harasser may get to the point of putting their arm around you, touching your shoulder, or patting your buttocks while walking past you. These are all signs that you are dealing with a sensitive and potentially dangerous situation. It is not a situation to ignore. So what do you do if this happens to you?

The first thing you should do is take the issue to the company human resources department. If there is no such department at your place of employment, then you need to meet with the owner or top executive of the company. Next, you may have to contact an attorney so you can put your issues in front of someone who can protect and defend you if necessary. The other obvious thing to do is stay as far away from the harasser as possible. I recognize that this may be difficult given that you work for this person. You may have to resign in order to protect yourself from the unwanted advances of your boss. If you do this, then make sure you do so in a written format with all the pertinent details of the sexual harassment, and give the letter to the owner or even someone in charge of human resources of the company with a copy being sent to an attorney.

Working in an environment where you are subjected to sexual harassment is not something to take lightly. There have been circumstances where harassment has turned into violence, and where a superior may make suggestions that your employment depends upon you following through with sexual favors. Should you find yourself in this kind of scenario you need to take immediate action to protect yourself from further potential harm both professionally and personally. Again, it is not something to take lightly or to ignore.

There is another scenario that deals with sexual harassment in the workplace and this is when your boss suggests to you that you take one for the team. What does this comment mean? This might arise when a customer is making lewd suggestions to you, and hints that the business that they provide to your company is dependent upon you providing some kind of sexual favor. Your boss, who indicates to you that you should take one for the team, suggests that it is incumbent upon you to do whatever it takes to retain the business of this particular customer. This is a blatant example of harassment by your boss and by the customer. Neither is acceptable, and you should take immediate steps to surface this issue to the owner or top leader of the company.

THE SECRETS KEEPER

This is the kind of boss that hides things from you that are integral to your ability to do your job well. Your boss may be someone who is suspicious of you and your ability to move up the ladder at work. They may see you as a threat to their own position and livelihood. If so, they may try to make things difficult for you by assigning projects of great importance to the company, but simultaneously withholding key bits of information that makes completion of your assignment virtually impossible. They are malicious in their intent and they take these steps knowing full well what they mean.

If your boss is the owner of the company this would generally not occur, however if the owner is looking for a way to get rid of you, then they may take these kinds of steps to make you look bad and then fire you for poor performance. The best way to deal with this kind of situation is of course to never allow it to occur in the first place. So how would you do this?

The ideal way to deal with a potential lack of essential information is to make sure that you set the correct set of expectations *up front* before a project takes place. This may include a *set of parameters* in terms of goals and objectives. It may include expenditures and limits to your project costs. It may include an *outline of the necessary information* that is required to complete the project in entirety. It may include *timing limits and expectations*. If you can get all of this down in writing then you have hopefully limited the possibility for your boss or owner to create a no-win situation for you.

There are many owners and top managers that prefer to keep certain aspects of their company confidential. This should not be construed in the same sense of secret keeping, because the company is a privately held entity, entitled to certain privacy rights. If they want to maintain secrecy about the financial condition of their company, then that is their right and privilege. If they want to refuse information that is necessary for you to do your job, then that is not acceptable. It may be their right, but it does not make them right. You need to be able to ascertain what information you need in order to perform your job to the specifications and requirements that were originally communicated to you when you first took the job.

THROWING YOU AN ANCHOR

Perhaps one day you will find yourself receiving what appears to be a fantastic opportunity by your boss or owner of the company. They will approach you with a new idea and they have chosen you to lead the project. Wow, you say to yourself! This is great! What you don't realize, however, is that you have just been thrown an anchor, an anchor which will inevitably drown you in failure. Why would someone do this to you?

If you are thrown an anchor it will be an act that is many times premeditated in nature, but sometimes it is done unknowingly because the outcome is a surprise to everyone. In the first case you may be on the losing end of some kind of decision that was meant to oust you from the company, and this was the mechanism the owner or boss decided to use. In the second case, you will hopefully be given the benefit of the doubt when things end up being deemed a failure. In either case you will want to determine upfront what the motivation is for the owner or manager to make the decision to give you the opportunity to lead this new project.

There are cases where the anchor being thrown is not an intentional act meant to oust you from the company, but where it ends up happening anyway. Let's use an example to help understand that kind of outcome.

A SURVIVAL GUIDE ON WORKING FOR A FAMILY OWNED COMPANY

Let's say that you have done a great job of managing one of several fast food franchise stores. Your store is outperforming all of the others. The owner of all of these stores comes to you one day and says that they need you to take over as manager of the worst producing store. The performance at that store is undercutting the value of the entire franchise network and they need you to fix the problem. You view this not only as a challenge, but you also feel that this request means that your value to the company has grown significantly. So you take over as manager of the new store, and meanwhile your assistant manager at your old store takes over as manager of your previous highest producing store.

Three months goes by and the results at your new store have not yet improved. During this same time frame the results at your old store have managed to hit record high revenues and profits for each of the three successive months. You hear through the grapevine that the owner is infatuated with your old protégé that took over your previous store. All of a sudden you are feeling worried and vulnerable. You sense that there may be no going back to where you were before, and that maybe you have been handed an anchor of a situation. This is a case where all of your good work in the past has managed to put you in a situation where you may end up looking like the loser in this managerial switcheroo. Was it planned to work out this way? The answer is, probably not, but it is what it is, and you are now feeling a sense of desperation. You begin to make decisions at your new store that are out of character for you, and the results start to worsen. Within two months the owner decides to close the store and you and everyone working there is let go. You are at a loss for words, but you are also unemployed. How would you have prevented this from happening?

Prior to your move to the new store you should have talked with the owner or your boss about the possibility of the situation not working out. Maybe the store was destined to fail regardless of who the manager was at the time. Perhaps it was in the wrong location. Perhaps the wages were too high based on area wage schedule and competition. Perhaps it was underfunded from the start. Your objective at the time was to ensure that your prior efforts and accomplishments were never to be forgotten, and that your employment opportunities would not end if things were to fail for reasons beyond your control. In addition, you should have made sure that you had *all of this in writing* so that your employment would not come to an end.

There are many intricacies in the world of business, and it's impossible to predict or fathom them all, but it is imperative that you give due consideration and investigation to every aspect of every opportunity that comes your way. Some of them will be long-lasting and beneficial in nature. Some of them, however, may be anchors that will drag you down into an abyss of unemployment.

TOO MUCH FEEDBACK

This kind of boss or owner is guilty of talking to you too much and providing you with too much information. This may come about by virtue of your boss becoming too chummy from a personal standpoint; or it can happen when your boss comes close to actually doing your job for you; or it can arise from your boss telling you about other employees in the organization. This is the type of situation where the owner or boss is either reluctant to let go of their decision making authority, or where the owner or boss is far too involved from a personal perspective with all of the employees, not just you.

In fact, maybe the boss is telling other employees about you, not just from a work standpoint, but also from a personal perspective. They are far too close to far too many people, and for whatever reason they just can't seem to keep their trap shut. They start rumoring to virtually everyone about everyone else. This becomes a toxic environment to work in due to all of the rumors and the aftermath of backbiting that takes place. Sooner rather than later the entire workplace becomes a cesspool of unfounded information and predictable distrust, leading to a totally dysfunctional company.

Many employees do want additional feedback from their boss and/or owner. They want to know exactly what they're doing right and what they're doing wrong. They feel that the more they know and the sooner they know it, the better off they will be in terms of stable employment. There is a degree of truth to this perspective. If you as an employee hear no feedback, then you might start to worry about your job stability. In some cases, employees who hear nothing from their supervisor start to take things for granted and eventually begin making unauthorized decisions or decisions that lead to unfortunate events. I can understand the need for timely feedback, as long as it doesn't occur all day long or every day of the week.

Owners or bosses that are suspicious of their employees are far more likely to overstep the fine line boundary between boss and employee. They primarily do this because of their insecurity with other people in general, and they then have a tendency to check and double check everything that others do. They end up looking over everyone's shoulders and second guessing every decision or action made by their employees. This kind of overreach is unhealthy for the organization, for the owner, for your boss, and for you. Most employees want some leeway in their ability to make decisions and carry out their duties. I think they appreciate some constructive feedback, but not the kind of browbeating interference that this kind of boss carries out on a daily basis.

As a final thought on this topic, the vast majority of employees want to succeed at their job by virtue of *their own initiative* and performance. They do not want their boss or owner doing their job form them. What they do want is honest feedback that tells them whether they are on the right or wrong track. They want the support of their boss, but not their boss taking over their responsibilities. Too much feedback, whether it's personal or professional, is not good for any employee.

TOO LITTLE FEEDBACK

This kind of boss or owner almost never talks to you. They don't talk about your work or your personal life. It's almost as if you didn't exist at all, except for the fact that you actually do. You have a job at their company, yet the boss or manager doesn't take the time to speak with you.

This boss or manager is most likely someone who is not only secure with their ability to hire the right people, but also in their obsession with running their business strategically while allowing their employees to each do their own job. This managerial philosophy is probably great for the company as a whole, but maybe not as great for you. Not getting any feedback about your job performance is not a good thing for anyone. You need some periodic performance reviews and some degree of direction, perhaps not on a day to day basis, but certainly weekly or monthly. No dialogue at all from your boss or owner leaves you wondering about your overall status and value to the organization.

Should you find yourself in this situation you should find a way to ask the owner or your boss for a face to face meeting. Your purpose for the meeting is to express your desire for some job performance feedback from your boss. It does not have to be a long meeting, just time enough to say what you have to say and express your feelings to the boss. You want periodic feedback, that's all. You can explain to your boss that you feel somewhat insecure in your position when you get no feedback at all. Tell them that you enjoy your job, your work and the company, and that you have a desire to keep working there long into the future. In order to do so you would like some degree of feedback. Ask, don't demand, an answer to your request. Hopefully you will get the answer you want and deserve, and your professional life will get back on a normal track.

FORGETTING TO INCLUDE YOU

You might remember the movie, *Home Alone*, about a young boy being accidently forgotten, and left home alone during the Christmas holidays. The family had left for a vacation in Europe and the boy's mom finally remembered they had left him behind while on the airplane over the Atlantic Ocean. All out bedlam soon followed.

Bosses and owners are people too, and sometimes they have memory lapses just like the rest of us. Some will forget accidently, as in the movie mentioned above. Others may forget to include you in important matters and meetings with a purpose in mind. Maybe they don't want to include you for a reason, but why would they want to do such a thing?

There are times when a boss may elect not to include you in something if they believe your presence or input is unnecessary. That would be their prerogative. Sometimes they might not invite you to participate because you perhaps caused a stir of sorts in a previous get together. Maybe they regard you as somewhat of a troublemaker. That is also their prerogative, especially if the troublemaker part is true. Or maybe the boss doesn't forget to invite you, but they just want to find more ways to ease you out of the company. Maybe they want to purposely irritate you.

It's up to you as the employee to figure out why your boss or owner is making the decision to not include you in matters of importance and meetings. When you start to notice that your peers are getting invited but not you, then you have something to be concerned about. The questions for you are, one, why were you not invited, and two, what are you going to do about it? The quick answer is - ask! Ask your boss or owner why you were left out of the meeting or function or whatever conference call was going on. You don't necessarily deserve an answer but you would like one nevertheless.

I had a boss of mine years ago who would have periodic conference calls on a variety of subjects. Sometimes they would have all of the direct reports on the phone at the same time, and other times there were just a few. No one really ever asked why some people were left off certain calls. In fact I never asked either, so shame on me for not doing so. If I had to look back now and guess as to why certain people were left off certain calls, I would have to say that there had to be some purpose for doing so. I don't think it was accidental or an oversight of sorts, or that people just had something better to do at those times. There had to be an underlying reason for selecting who was on what call and on what days.

My boss at the time had their favorites; their favorite direct reports; their favorite employees; their favorite cities. I guess in and of itself that might not be so bad or so unusual in the world of business. What was unusual was the selection of participants based on what the end result of the call was designed to accomplish. I suspect that particular participants were selected based on the exact nature of what decision could be carried forth without a lot of dissention from the ranks. That sounds a bit like of an end around, where you are sneaking your way into a decision that you have already made in your own mind. You don't want anyone to muck it up, so you only invite those people that you know will follow your directives. This method of forgetting to include you is not healthy for the organization as a whole, and certainly not to you if you're one of the people being left out in the cold.

Remember at all times that everyone makes mistakes. Some people make them more often than others. That is not a crime by any means. But you will have to be on the lookout for the boss or owner who makes it a habit, a bad habit, of forgetting to include you on matters that you know should include you. When that kind if event occurs, you then have to decide how to best handle that situation, and determine the reasons for those forgetful moments.

SETTING YOU UP TO FAIL

Beware the boss or owner that decides to make sure that your departure from the company comes sooner rather than later. One might ask why they would hire you at all if their objective is to remove you from the payroll, but there are instances where the owner in question is not the person that hired you. Let's use an example of something that happened to a friend of mine many years ago.

She was hired by one of the owners of the company and it was clear from the very beginning that one of the other owners was totally against the idea of her employment. In fact, this second owner in question made a comment that made it crystal clear that they were not a fan of her hiring. In retrospect she is still not sure what the issue was at the time, but in any event something triggered this person's decision to attempt to set her up to fail. She knew this was going to happen, and so she was able to deflect and defer a lot of the noise that this owner sent her way in an attempt to undermine her success.

As time went on it became clear that her success was not going to be eroded by this person's underhanded tactics. One day she decided that it was time to go in a different direction, as she had another offer on the table from a competitor. She talked to her direct supervisor about the decision, and then something very odd happened. She received a call from this second owner in question, you know, the one that didn't want anything to do with her at the time of her hiring. Within minutes what she was hearing was how much she was valued by the company and by this owner in particular, and that she was now being offered a promotion along with a 25% pay increase and a guaranteed year-end bonus of 20% of her new base salary. WTF is this she thought at the time? Was she dreaming or was this for real?

Well, it was for real and she decided to stay the course and remain with the company. This same person who told her flat out that she was not their choice early on, was now her champion for the future? It was indeed hard to fathom what happened at the time, but she learned a year or two later why there was a change in heart. It turned out that the decision was based on an overriding business need whereby her departure would not have looked good internally and even more so externally. So much for the leopard changing spots; the spots were still there, they were just hidden at the time.

While this scenario worked out okay for my friend at the time, there are many instances in the workplace where an owner or boss makes a decision to set an employee up to fail. Maybe they think they made the wrong choice in hiring you in the first place. Maybe they decide they just don't like you personally. Maybe they think you're smarter than they are, and they want you out of their way. When any of these situations occur it is difficult to find a way around them.

It's not easy to determine just when or how or why a boss or owner comes to the conclusion that they do, but you will want to be very aware of changes in attitude and discourse in terms of how the owner interacts with you. The changes may be slight at first, but you will eventually notice that there is a pattern developing, and it is at that time that you will want to either address the matter head on, or start looking for an exit strategy. Overcoming a boss's desire to oust you from the company is almost impossible to counter. You may have some degree of legal ability to hang on to your job, but in the end this kind of owner will find a way to set you up to fail in order to terminate you for cause.

THE PROMOTER

This kind of boss or owner might be your dream boss, the kind of person who turns out to be your number one advocate in the company. Obviously you would have to be an excellent employee in order for this boss to hold you in such high regard. If you fit this prototype then you are in for what could be a great career path. Having a champion in your corner is a wonderful benefit and you should be careful to treat this kind of boss or owner with nothing but the highest regard.

I once had a boss like this and it worked out well in some regard and no so well in another regard. For some reason this boss thought of me as some sort of firefighter who could both extinguish flames of failure in various business units and thereafter resurrect those business units into future winners. This boss promoted me time and again; sometimes more frequently than what would or maybe even should be considered normal. The good news was that I managed to have some success at every stop along the journey. The bad news was that these moves took a tremendous toll on my personal life and my family at the time.

You would be wise to keep my journey in mind if and when you find yourself in a situation where your boss becomes a sort of full time mentor, and they begin to promote you into ever bigger jobs and at a rapid pace. Your boss in this case becomes a promoter, your personal promoter, and this can have both good and bad outcomes. Just be sure that you carefully think through every opportunity that is presented to you before you make any kind of decision. You should never make on the spot decisions of consequence without thinking and talking things through with third parties. If you have a family, then you certainly need to talk to your spouse and children, and maybe even your parents, and make sure everyone gets to have an opinion on the subject matter at hand.

You may find that your promoter of a boss or owner has ulterior motives for putting you on a fast track, so-to-speak. You need to figure this out quickly because if this is the case your promotion opportunity may be nothing more than a manipulative ruse. Maybe it's a case of harassment or sexual harassment. Maybe it's a case of simple infatuation. Maybe it's a case of your boss putting you in a situation where you might be able to be easily manipulated into doing something that is improper or illegal. If you get promoted it is incumbent upon you to determine the legitimacy and accuracy of the event in order to protect your own career.

A promotion can be a wonderful thing for you. Your promoter of a boss or owner can turn out to be the best boss you will ever have. I hope you pursue the truth behind the promotion and I hope you make sure that you get everything related to the promotion in writing prior to accepting the new role. Putting things in writing that are signed off on by your boss or better yet the owner is your way of protecting yourself as you progress through the ranks of your company.

A SURVIVAL GUIDE ON WORKING FOR A FAMILY OWNED COMPANY

WHEN YOUR BOSS IS THE OWNER

The good thing about your boss being the owner is that you know exactly who's calling the shots. If your boss is the owner, then that person calls the shots on hiring you, giving you direction on a daily basis, mentoring you, promoting you, giving you raises, and terminating you if necessary. There is no go-between to worry about, and for the most part whatever the owner says is the last word on all issues within the company.

I always liked working directly for the owner because I knew I could get quick answers and decisions, and I would never have to be concerned about the chain of command. The owner is in command of everything and everyone (more or less). If you are hired by the owner then you know who it is that you are beholden to (not totally though) and who you need to impress. If you get hired by a fast food franchisee owner and you start out by cleaning the cooking area and learning how to do minor repairs, you realize from day one that you need to learn everything you can about your first set of responsibilities in order to get a chance to move up the food chain so-to-speak. You have one person to impress, right?

Wrong! Yes, you have to impress the owner, but you also have to learn how to get along with everyone else working in that particular environment. If you manage to impress the owner but everyone else in the restaurant thinks you're an asshole, then you're not going to get very far. Every organization has a structure and every organization needs to have team players. The team is like a well-oiled machine - if the parts stop working together as they should or break down when they shouldn't, then the machine stops working. The same holds true for every company out there. Teamwork is paramount to success in today's world of business.

If the owner is your boss you have a better chance of making a nice career for yourself if you like the company and your job. However, if you fail to measure up to the owner's standards then you will also find yourself being quickly shown the exit door. Owners tend to take their business very seriously, and they general will not tolerate slackers, goof-offs, clock watchers, late arrivers, rules violators, time wasters, rumor mongers, or poor performers. Their company is their baby to a degree and they will not put up with a lot of nonsense. You had better be on your best behavior when you start working for the owner of a business.

In one of the last subchapters I mentioned some of the pitfalls that might come with working directly for the owner. If the owner is someone who takes advantage of people then you may have a problem on your hands. They could take advantage of your time, your resources, your knowledge and ability, and maybe even your body in the case of a harasser. In a family owned company where you are working directly for the owner you have no one further up the ladder to complain to. A mischievous owner could try taking advantage of you because they have done so to others in the past and gotten away with it, or they are trying to get you to do something in the future that would be beneficial to them. You need to be extremely careful to analyze what kind of owner you are working for in order to protect yourself.

I have worked directly for several owners and for the most part all of my relationships from a professional standpoint were quite positive. I consider myself fortunate that everything worked out as well as it did, and I am thankful for their mentorship. A good owner can really help make your career, so you will always want to create an above board relationship and keep that owner as a long term positive reference for yourself.

A SURVIVAL GUIDE ON WORKING FOR A FAMILY OWNED COMPANY

WHEN YOUR BOSS IS THE OWNER OR MANAGER'S KID

Beware the pitfalls of this kind of working relationship. You might find yourself working for the owner or manager's kid if the company is larger in size and the owner is getting older. In cases like this the owner or manager is looking to bring the kid along and up the ranks so that one day in the future the kid might be ready to take over the reins from the owner or manager as the new leader. All of that is just fine for the owner or manager and the kid, but it might not be so fine for the employees that need to work for the kid.

Now I want to make it clear that there are many, many companies out there where the boss's kid or kids are exemplary people who are a sheer joy to work for directly. Hopefully you will be lucky enough to be employed in such an environment. I know that I have experienced one such episode myself, and it was a relationship that I cherished for years. Others are not so fortunate.

There are some owner's kids out there who view their role to be somewhat of a ball buster because their tenure with the company is protected by virtue of their familial situation. This kind of boss is toxic to the entire organization. They enjoy tearing people down and making an example of them in plain sight of other employees. They do this because they can, and because it feeds their ego and their need for displaying power. If you find yourself working for one of these kids you might want to see if you can transfer to another job that doesn't report to this kid.

Then there are situations where there is more than just one kid working in the company. Let's say that there are two of the owner's kids working in the company, and you work for one of them. I've heard of several situations in the past where the two kids had somewhat of an adversarial relationship inside the company, with each of them picking and choosing which employees they could persuade to be on their team. This kind of scenario creates a deep divide inside the owner's company, and sometime the owner doesn't even notice what's going on for quite some time. When the owner does finally realize the impact, they are at a loss as to how to best solve the problems that have been created. The owner can become hesitant to make any decision that may alienate one of the kids, or create an even more toxic relationship than already exists.

I mentioned in another chapter the pitfalls that are involved when your boss is one of the owner's kids, and the kid begins to hint at developing more of a personal relationship than a business relationship. Sometimes this kind of issue can work out just fine, but most of the time it can become an albatross around your neck because the kid will begin to take undue advantage of the personal side of the equation. Later on, when the kid finally moves up the ladder into a more senior position, or even the top position, your relationship may become an issue that they want to rid themselves of. If that happens then you may find yourself looking for a new job. The key to all of this is to tread lightly when working for the owner's kids. Keep it on a business level and refrain from letting the relationship get out of hand.

In the next chapter we will focus on how to survive business meetings. We all realize that meetings are part of conducting business and they are a norm that just won't go away. How to behave in meetings is another matter. What to say and when to say it and who to say it to are all quandaries that need to be addressed. Meetings can make or break your career in many ways, and we will look carefully at some of the pitfalls to avoid. We will also look at several ideas on how to put your best foot forward before, during and after meetings. You will always want to be *better prepared than anyone else.*

CHAPTER EIGHT
SURVIVING BUSINESS MEETINGS

Business meetings seem to be a staple of day to day company management whether the company is small, medium or large, and regardless of industry or ownership. Why are meetings so important and is there a possibility that they can be eliminated? Meetings are a mechanism for sharing information from the top down, in other words a time and place for the owner or top management to disseminate important information or data with company leadership or with all employees in the case of a smaller entity. Of course in today's world much of this could be achieved via email, but most members of upper management or ownership prefer a face to face type environment so they are able to gauge responsiveness and acceptance to whatever their message might be. It's also a forum that allows for questions and answers.

Meetings are also a means by which leadership and employees alike can *strategize and problem solve as a team*. This type of scenario is valuable for the company's long term success and enables the ownership to engrain and support meaningful employee contributions toward the future. Meetings can also take place with lower management levels within the organization, and can also take place with just employees and no management present. These types of meetings can help solve a variety of day to day issues as opposed to more *strategic* issues.

Any time there is a meeting there is of course the chance for agreement and disagreement. Everyone has an opinion on most everything, and most meetings are meant to give everyone at the meeting a chance to express their opinions about whatever the subject matter might be at that time. Sometimes disagreements can turn into constructive dialogue and eventual agreement, however sometimes they also turn into verbal shouting matches and stronger disagreement. This is a downside of meetings for sure, and a situation that no one wants or enjoys. It is not constructive and can lead to internal dissent that lingers into the future.

Meetings can produce answers and meetings can also produce a lack of future focus by virtue of indecision and disagreement. Every meeting should have an agenda, a time frame, a methodology for information sharing and opinions, and an objective or outcome that can declare the meetings successful or unsuccessful. Meetings should not end up being a waste of time for the participants, and unfortunately many meetings turn out just that way, which then leaves the attendees muttering to themselves afterward. In that kind of situation the participants then begin to feel frustration about meetings in general, and that spells a bad trend for the future.

There are certain *protocols* for every meeting, and everyone should be aware of who is in charge and leading the meeting. The leader of every meeting should open the meeting with a short overview of the meeting agenda, time frame, outcome and process for information sharing. The leader needs to monitor the time limits on discussion of all topics and make sure that the meeting discussions stay on topic at all times. It is far too easy for participants to veer off target and start talking about things that are not germane to the primary meeting topic and outcome. This will make the meeting longer and less productive, and the leader needs to rein people in if and when this occurs.

This chapter is designed to highlight some of the more important aspects of employee behavior during meetings, and exactly how participants can best prepare for their own involvement. Every employee who is involved with a meeting needs to be aware of the pitfalls that can occur, and the opportunities that are sometimes presented. Careers can be made or broken by virtue of how you handle yourself during a company meeting.

MEETING TIME

Someone sets the start time for every meeting, and that someone should be the leader who called the meeting. This could be the owner, another executive in the company, or even an employee team leader. Regardless of who calls the time, the important thing for any participant is to be at the right place for the meeting and to be on time every time. In my book *being on time means being early*, every time. If the meeting starts at 8 a.m. then being on time means being there at 7:55 a.m. or earlier. On time is not 8:01 or 8:05. Never be late for a meeting, not for any reason. If you think you're going to be late then you're better off getting hold of the leader who called the meeting and beg forgiveness for missing the meeting, and provide a damn good excuse for doing so. But at least you won't be late!

Meeting times are set in such a way that the activities of the meeting are meant to begin at precisely the time of the meeting. That means if the meeting starts at 8 a.m. the leader will begin opening remarks at that time and not a minute later. If you walk in at 8:02 then you are going to miss the remarks of the leader, and worse yet, your walking in late will cause a disruption to those remarks, making for a very awkward moment for you and everyone else. Do you really want to get the evil eye from all of your peers and the meeting leader? Suppose the leader is actually your boss or the owner? How do you think that will affect you in the future?

I have personally been involved in lots of meetings in the past, some of which I was the leader who called the meeting and many others where I was an invited participant. I have seen all kinds of circumstances where someone walked into the meeting late. It was never good and never acceptable to me or most anyone else. I've seen people walk in a minute late, and some fifteen minutes late. How do you explain being fifteen minutes late for a meeting? Your car broke down? You got caught in traffic? Your watch is wrong? You thought the meeting was tomorrow or at a different time? You got delayed on a call with a client? Maybe one of these or maybe each of these is an acceptable excuse to you, but none of them will be acceptable to the leader of the meeting and certainly not to your boss or the owner.

Remember the 7"P"'s that I talked about in some of the earlier chapters? Let me remind you of the meaning - Proper Prior Planning Prevents Piss Poor Performance. Each of the excuses for being late to a meeting that are noted above can be *prevented by planning ahead*. If your car broke down you probably noticed something wrong earlier and decided not to pay attention to getting the problem fixed. If you got caught in traffic then you didn't check traffic volume or leave early enough. Your watch is wrong if you never set it right or change the battery when you should have done so. The client call could have been deferred until after the meeting. In other words you were late and you were also negligent in doing everything you could to prevent it from occurring.

Being late for a meeting can be further aggravated by doing any of the following - showing up drunk or slurring your words; showing up late and then talking nonstop after doing so; ignoring the leader and failing to apologize for being late; sitting down and starting to talk to other attendees; failing to bring a writing pad or notebook and pen or pencil to take notes; eating while walking in to the meeting; ogling at another of the meeting participants or sending hand written personal notes to other participants; continuing to eat during the meeting when no one else has food; slurping your coffee or some other drink; mocking the meeting leader by making faces or laughing; and looking at the clock or your watch all the time as if you have somewhere else to be at this time. Any of these transgressions will cost you dearly in employee bonding and endearment to the leader, your boss or the owner.

KNOW YOUR STUFF

Every meeting should have an agenda published in advance, along with a list of attendees. If your name is on the list of participants there is a reason. Maybe you're one of the leader's direct reports and all of your peers are there. Maybe you are involved with a particular project that is being discussed at the meeting. Maybe all of the employees have been invited, which is normally the case in a smaller size company. In any case there is a reason for your attendance, which means you *better be prepared*.

Since you have been apprised of the agenda in advance you should have been studying or researching everything you could have about the specifics of the topic. It is imperative that when the discussions turn to you for your input, you are properly prepared to provide specific answers, suggestions or recommendations. Getting caught flat footed with no real valuable answers will most certainly mean that you were ill prepared or that you didn't prepare at all. It will get noticed by your peers and by your boss, the owner and the meeting leader.

Let's say that you are called to a meeting and the subject matter is a lack of profitability in your particular division of the company. You are one of the lower level leaders of this division and as such you have some degree of responsibility for producing profits for the division. So, you know the topic and you know that you have a degree of responsibility for the problem at hand. In advance of the meeting you should be studying financial statements that pertain to your division and in particular your area within the division. You will need to be prepared to give answers to questions about why the division is not achieving the planned profits. You will need reasons for the poor performance and recommendations as to how to fix the issues at hand. You can only do this by doing your homework ahead of time.

I can tell you that if you fail to provide answers when called upon to do so, you will risk your own position within the company. Remember that your position presumably has some accountability for providing profits. If you can't deliver the needed results then your boss or the owner is likely to find someone else who can deliver the necessary profit numbers. Being prepared is incredibly important for this reason, and also to keep pace with your peers in the company. You don't want to look bad in front of your peers, as that will increase their standing inside the company and simultaneously diminish your own standing.

Another example of a reason for a meeting might be a process problem. Let's say that you are working at a bakery and the owner is calling a meeting to discuss why the shop is running out of the proper amount of a particular pastry ingredient. The owner has noticed that the product has been a good seller lately but that by Thursday of the last few weeks the store has not been able to keep up with the demand for the pastry product. Since weekends are normally the best time frame for sales, customers have begun to file a higher than normal amount of complaints about the lack of this pastry product. The owner is losing customers and you are called in as part of the team that has responsibility for process delivery.

In this kind of situation you better have looked into the reasons for this problem, and you better have details and solutions. Do not just gloss over any facts that you come across. The more details you have the better the outcome will be for solving the problem, and the more informed you will look to peers, the boss and the owner. Do your homework and really dig into the whys and wherefores of the issue. Talk to other employees who are involved. Talk to the suppliers that your company deals with for this pastry problem. Ask lots of questions and dig for answers. This is an opportunity for you to shine, so don't pass it up.

BE PREPARED FOR SURPRISES

What kind of surprises, you might be asking right now? No, I don't think you will all of a sudden be bombarded with balloons and confetti for a surprise birthday party or work anniversary, although that's not totally improbable. That is not the kind of surprise I'm talking about here. I'm also not talking about some announcement about an employee get together after work that night, or some employee outing later in the month. Those might be nice surprises to hear about, but they are not relevant to this discussion topic.

First off, if you're not properly prepared for the meeting the surprise you might get is to be told by the meeting leader that you are excused from the meeting forthwith. What that means in business lingo is to get the hell out of the room and do it now! Do not pass go and collect $200 as in Monopoly. Just head straight for the door and don't come back. How's that for a surprise? Ah, you don't like that one? Well then, try this one on for size.

You walk into the meeting with all of your peers present, and the owner or manager stands up to address everyone. They do not look happy and all of a sudden you get a big knot in your stomach. You're beginning to wonder if there's bad news coming soon. The owner or manager looks around the room one by one and stares into everyone's eyes. Now you're feeling tense and you're almost afraid to move. You see that others have the same feeling. Then the announcement comes. The leader tells everyone that the company is not doing well financially. Something needs to be done they say, or the company may have to close. Several moments pass with no one saying anything. You can hear a pin drop it's so quiet. Now that's a surprise you don't ever want to hear, right? Of course you don't. but if you're *paying attention to details on a day to day basis*, then this announcement wouldn't necessarily be a total surprise, would it? You would see or hear things that may lead you to have an idea that the company was having some difficulties. You would be prepared for this kind of announcement.

Another surprise you might not expect is that your boss tells everyone that they are leaving for a new job with a different company. That's it; just like that you get word that the person who has perhaps been your mentor will be gone at the end of the day. Wow, you're thinking to yourself! Now that's a surprise. You didn't see that one coming at all, and it's going to happen at the end of today; no notice you think; what's up with that, you ask yourself quietly? Do you think that can't happen? Well I can assure you that it can and most likely will at some point during your career. People do change jobs, some more than others, so put yourself in the frame of mind right now that it's going to happen to you at some point. Instead of being surprised, just be ready when it does occur.

Surprises come in all sizes and categories, so-to-speak. Some can impact you personally, like a change in your salary or a change in your company benefits. Other more personal changes can impact your job function, or perhaps even a promotion or demotion. Maybe the owner or manager will tell you that the company has been bought by another company and the new owners have indicated that there will be a workforce reduction as a result of the sale. It might include you, but there are no real details at this juncture. Maybe the owner or manager will tell everyone that the company is not being sold, but they have decided to relocate the entire company to a different city and even a different state. That sounds like it could be personal in nature. Moving for the job, seriously? Are you ready for that one? No, then get ready because it can and has happened many times over. All businesses can be personal, and the only one that gets to make that kind of decision is the owner or top executive. You do get to decide if you want to move; that is, if you're even asked to move and remain with the company.

The point of this subchapter is to elevate your inner sense of not liking to be surprised so that in effect you are better prepared for surprises when they actually do occur. Surprises, like it or not, are part of the business culture and your career will be better served by knowing this in advance.

BRINGING FOOD

Everyone likes food, right? Well, most everyone that is. Some of us are pickier eaters than others, and others are maybe on a diet or fasting or some other form of personalized eating behavior. Some people like meat and others are vegetarians. Some people are lactose intolerant and others love a good milkshake or ice cream sundae. Some people like their coffee black and others like cream or cream and sugar. The bottom line is that people have different tastes and one size does not fit all when it comes to food.

There are many companies and many meeting leaders that not only allow food at meetings, but that actually promote and encourage doing so. They do this because people like food and sharing food together, as in dining together, and it promotes a sense of teamwork and personal interaction. What meeting leaders do not want, however is a mess on the conference room table, a food fight that turns ugly, or people eating and not paying attention to the actual reason for the meeting. No one likes to see you eating at a meeting and seeing food come slithering out of your mouth, or to see you spit your food out all over the table or yourself or others. There is a limit to what you can and can't do when eating food at a meeting, so be very aware of your own actions more so than the actions of others.

Generally the meeting leader will either designate one of the meeting attendees to arrange for all of the food for a meeting, or they may do the arranging themselves or ask an assistant to do so on their behalf. Most meetings that involve food being brought into the workplace are either first thing in the morning or around the lunch hour. The next few paragraphs will focus on what your role should include if you are the designated meeting attendee in charge of bringing the food. Bringing food can offer you great kudos and benefits from your peers and boss or owner, or it can result in an all-out shellacking of your ability to cater meeting events. Let's examine the breakfast meeting and then the lunch meeting opportunities.

Your meeting leader, and remember this could be your boss or owner, designates you to handle breakfast duties for a meeting to take place next week. The meeting will start promptly at 8:30 a.m. in the conference room and the number of attendees will be eight people, all of whom are peers of yours. Peers, just to be clear, are those employees who either hold the same job title that you do or they have a role that is on the same level in an organization chart. You don't want to drop the ball with the food responsibility because you may become the laughing stock of the meeting. Let me give you an example of something that actually happened in one of the meetings that I held years ago.

I decided to hold a sales meeting at 8:30 a.m., and the attendees were all the salespeople in the company. They were peers of one another. I assigned one of the salespeople to bring the food and they accepted the challenge. This employee decided that they were going to bring in donuts for everyone, as well as coffee and assorted items. This employee, in their infinite wisdom, decided to purchase the donuts the evening prior to the meeting, presumably to save time the next morning. I'm not sure that even that decision was a prudent one from the start, but to make matters worse they left the donuts in their car overnight. It was winter and it was cold, and when the donuts arrived at the meeting they were as hard as a rock. The attendees broke into a combination of hysterical laughter, lighthearted name calling, and outright ridicule. The designated employee turned crimson in color and begged for forgiveness while trying to explain the unexplainable. They never lived that moment down. The story became one that was told and retold many times over during that year or so time frame. The moral of this story should be self-evident to you. Be smart and don't try to take shortcuts.

The second example will be one involving bringing food for a lunch hour time frame meeting. Let's just stick with the same group of attendees that we discussed in the paragraphs above, and this meeting revolved around sales prospecting. I assigned one person to handle the food chores and they decided it would be pizza, a not so bad choice for a meeting at that time of day. Here is the problem that they created without thinking about all of the details. This person decided to order the pizza, but instead of having it delivered, they made the choice to go pick it up at the pizza shop and bring it back. So far, not a huge mistake, but it became one when on the way to the pick-up they ran into a freight train that delayed all of the traffic. The delay in waiting for the train to pass cost this person a good fifteen minutes in time. This led to their arriving for the pick-up about thirty minutes past when the pizza was to be ready. By the time they got back to the meeting the pizza had been sitting for forty-five minutes. The pizza was cold and it was a dismal failure for this assigned food person. No one enjoyed the pizza and the employee took a huge hit from their peers on their lack of planning. Once again the moral of the story is to be prudent when you have this type of responsibility, and don't take shortcuts. If you can have the food delivered please do so.

One more suggestion on this issue of food at a meeting - try to use a knife and a fork when eating. Eating with your hands isn't a pretty sight for anyone to observe from around the room. It leads to food slipping or dripping out of your mouth, and no one wants to see that happening. Display good table manners, despite not being at an actual table. This is especially important if your boss or the owner is in attendance at the meeting. Good social skills and etiquette are important tools to have and to exhibit if you have any chance at moving up the chain of command at your workplace. Think ahead about how you want to act in meetings in general, and especially in meetings that involve food. Your behavior will say a lot about who and what you are, and about your future prospects within the organization.

DON'T BE A CRITIC

Meetings can unfortunately be a time when some people lose their temper or their cool, and they become a cancer inside and during the meeting. Meeting leaders, bosses and owners are not fans of behavior that stymies positive discussions and desired outcomes. Attendees that exhibit critical behavior towards the leader or boss or owner will develop an almost instantaneous reputation for being a future unwanted participant. People who are designated as critics are seen as people who think they know more than anyone else. They are seen as egotists and self-serving individuals.

You know who critics are, right? You can see them in newspapers where they are dissecting every word and every action of some politician, or you can see them in the arts section trying to tell you how or why you should or shouldn't go see a particular movie. These are people who are paid to be critics. You, as an employee of the company, are not being paid to be a critic of the company or of anyone in the company. You are being paid to be a constructive agent of change (if change is necessary), and to act accordingly without malice or judgmental temperament.

An especially egregious mistake that a meeting attendee can make is to create a firestorm of disagreement with the meeting leader or boss or owner that becomes overly critical in nature with regard to the strategic direction of the company. There are some owners or bosses who do not mind employee disagreements when handled with the utmost of professionalism. Then there are some owners and bosses who become insulted when anyone tries to critique their strategy or methodology. You will want to make sure that you take the time to figure out as quickly as possible which kind of boss or owner you are working for at your company. Taking the wrong approach and using the wrong tactics can be career killers almost instantaneously.

The key for you as an employee is to maintain a sense of constant decorum throughout any meetings that you are invited to attend. There is a right way and a wrong way to be critical of a process or a procedure or a strategy. The right way is to offer alternative solutions. The wrong way is to just criticize the issue without taking the appropriate steps to define recommendations for possible changes. Critics are viewed as argumentative. Solution providers are viewed as thoughtful and forward thinking. Which do you want to be remembered as during your tenure with your employer?

DON'T POINT FINGERS

This is an issue very similar to the one above where we discussed the pitfalls of being a critic. This problem arises when the meeting leader surfaces a particular problem within the company or the department, and you as an invited member of the meeting use the occurrence to directly accuse one of the other attendees as being the main culprit behind the problem. In fact there are occasions where someone may actually point their finger towards a particular person while simultaneously verbally attacking that person as the one responsible for the issue being discussed. This can cause severe repercussions for you as an employee and as an individual.

Accusatory behavior in a meeting of any kind is an unacceptable way to conduct yourself as a professional. The correct way to address problems is to define the issues at hand in some degree of detail, and to then perform a painstaking analysis of all the inner workings that can cause the problems. In essence what you do is a *cause and effect analysis* to figure out the root or roots of the problem. Taking aim at a particular person as the main cause of any particular problem is not the way to go. There may be cause to think that a particular person is the main cause, but even if that is the case in your mind, taking the step to point the finger directly at this person is a horrible method to employ.

I have seen moments in meetings that I attended in the past where the employee being accused with a pointed finger becomes completely unhinged and initiates a physical altercation in the meeting itself. When I saw this take place there was only one way to handle the issue, and that was to take appropriate action against both the parties; the first one for initiating the finger pointing and the second one for initiating the altercation. There is no excuse for either party behaving the way they did, but it can happen. Just don't let it happen to you.

Another way that people point fingers is to do so surreptitiously, meaning that they find a way to accuse people behind their back instead of out in the open at a meeting. This tactic may even be worse that the physical finger pointing because it can create additional disharmony within the organization. Let's say that after a meeting one of the attendees asks to talk with you on a confidential basis. You should immediately be suspicious of this kind of request. You have reservations but you finally agree to meet. This person tells you that there is someone in particular that is responsible for the problem that was discussed at the meeting, but they did not want to point fingers at the meeting itself. Now you have a quandary on your hands, because this person has involved you in their behind the scenes finger pointing, which makes you a sort of accomplice to the process.

What do you do with this information? Do you keep quiet and say nothing? Do you take the information and relay it to your boss or to the owner? Do you go to the person who has been accused and inform them of the finger pointing? What happens when the person who came to you tells others about the conversation, and then the owner finds out later that you knew but said nothing to anyone? Wow, there are not many good options on this kind of scenario. The right decision was to reject the initial offer of the secret meeting, and to tell them to take their information to the party who has the appropriate authority to best handle the issue at hand. Getting involved with any form of finger pointing is something you are best avoiding at all costs.

JAMES W. BENDER

BE A PROBLEM SOLVER

We've discussed the critics and the finger pointers, and now we will discuss the most appropriate way for you as a meeting attendee to be a *constructive* participant. It's by being a problem solver and not a problem creator. The leader of the meeting has most likely called the meeting to discuss a particular issue or a particular problem. You hope that the leader will first take the time to lay out the details of the issue or problem. You then hope that the leader asks for input from each of the meeting attendees. Everyone gets a chance to share their perspectives. That's the right way to handle a meeting.

It's finally your turn to offer your opinions. Instead of criticizing or pointing fingers, your tactic involves *suggestions and recommendations.* You have listened intently while the leader and others spoke, and you now have the opportunity to display the right way to handle the problem. You quietly and methodically introduce your suggestions to the group. You do not critique anyone or anything. You maintain a positive attitude and approach during your entire presentation. You are the consummate professional and you appear positive, level-headed and detailed in your outline of the issues and your recommendations. This methodology will win you friends among your peers and admiration from the leader, the boss or the owner.

Presenting solutions can be done more effectively with props. This might mean a flip chart where you can write and diagram as you speak. It might mean a hand-out that describes and depicts the details of your suggestions. It could also mean a computerized presentation like power point to take your audience through the details of your ideas on a point by point, page by page basis. Unfortunately this is not something that you can just pull out of your briefcase on a moment's notice. This is only something you can utilize if you have some advance notice of the issue to be discussed at the meeting. If you do get some early notice then you want to be ready to use your props. Maybe you can even ask the meeting leader for some inside help in order to best facilitate whatever you've decided to use as your prop methodology. Inside help in this case means some extra time or perhaps some help in getting the meeting room set up for your prop demonstration. Either way, your objective is to be prepared and professional in your approach to be a problem solver.

BE WARY OF GETTING DRAGGED INTO CONTROVERSIAL TOPICS

Meetings can be tricky at times. Let's say that someone brings up a subject matter that seemingly is outside the purview of the meeting leader and the overall rationale behind the meeting in general. The person that brought up this new issue may have an unseen agenda in mind. Maybe they are hoping that you or others at the meeting will say something that will either offend someone else, or maybe bring something up that others don't know about or need to know about, or maybe even say something negative about the boss or owner that will eventually get back to them and get you or someone else in hot water. The question will become this one - do you trust everyone in attendance at the meeting you are in?

I realize that you want to trust everyone, and I believe most people feel the same way. However, trust me when I tell you that there are many people in the world, including some of the people you work with an attend meetings with, that are not trustworthy. These are the type of individuals that might go to great lengths to drag you into a subject matter that is controversial in nature, and one that should not be discussed in a public forum such as a business meeting. This is the type of person who thrives on controversy and who enjoys getting people in trouble with the boss or owner. Let's look at a hypothetical example of something that could happen to you in today's world.

You are sitting in a meeting with a dozen or so peers from several different departments. The leader of the meeting is going through a series of financial reports that involve each of the departments. The leader mentions the new government mandate that will soon hike the minimum hourly wage to fifteen dollars per hour. They continue on about the potential impact on financial results for the company as a whole, and they start to talk about ways by which the company can counter the wage hikes. The conversation turns to others at the meeting, and several good ideas are presented. Suddenly one of the meeting attendees bursts out in a mini rant about Democrats ruining the country's business environment with all of their liberal leaning policies, including this now mandated wage hike. This person takes a short breath and then looks at you directly, asking you what your take is on the political atmosphere in the country. Now what do you do?

This is clearly an example of getting dragged into what could be a very controversial topic. Do you answer the question directly or at all for that matter? Do you wave off the query and try to send the conversation back toward the meeting leader? Do you stay focused on the actual subject matter of the meeting, which if financial results, and continue to explore new ideas for countering the wage increase? Do you say something back to the inquirer that is a bit of a reprimand for taking the conversation off course and into a dicey arena? Clearly there are a number of ways that you could handle this matter.

What you don't want to do is get dragged into a no-win situation, and politics in general is always a no-win situation, because everyone has their own opinions about political parties, politicians, party platforms, and a whole host of other dicey issues that are politically oriented. Wading into politics during a meeting is much like wading into politics at family gatherings. Nothing good can come from doing so. The only thing that can happen, and does happen, is additional internal friction between fellow employees or fellow family members. Situations such as these create hostility, bad blood, and a memory bank that is very hard to forget. People who drag you into this scenario are usually polarizing in nature as a general rule, and are normally people who have hard and fast ideas about almost everything, not just politics. They are also the type of people who have little regard for the feelings and opinions of others, so why bother taking the time to interact with them at all? The quick answer in my opinion is - don't do it.

Here is another example of getting dragged into a controversial subject while at a meeting. The owner or top executive of your company calls you and your particular peer group into a meeting to discuss hiring and compensation practices. The owner is concerned that their company is lagging in diversity and they want to find out why that is the case, and what the company can do to improve their overall diversity and compensation practices. Keep in mind here that it is the owner who has made the decision to improve diversity hiring and compensation practices in their company.

The owner or manager wants each member of this peer group to offer their individual perspectives on the subject at hand, more so from the standpoint of how to improve things than personal feelings. The first person to speak starts by remarking that one of their peers is absent from the meeting, and they wonder aloud why that is the case. They continue on by noting that the team member that is missing is the only female in the group, and further suggests that a meeting such as this one should include diversity. They ask whether it is appropriate to postpone this meeting until this female member can be present. Another long tenured peer group member blasts this idea as part of the reason the company is heading in the wrong direction. The suggestion is that everyone pays far too much attention to diversity and far too little attention to bottom line results. The owner or manager senses a brewing controversy and asks you what you think. Now what do you do?

Maybe you feel the same way about diversity that your leader does or maybe your feelings sway more toward the other peer member. You start to think whether you are being dragged into a more controversial subject that you first thought. First, keep in mind that your leader is the one that called this meeting and the subject matter, so it is obviously something that is important to them. Second, remember that the owner or manager is the person who either owns or has the ultimate responsibility for the company, so they get to call the shots on pretty much everything that goes on in their organization. Based on these two issues, your best bet is to stay the course with the owner or manager and suggest that everyone who is present could express their ideas on how to make improvements to diversity and compensation, and then the group could reconvene at a later date to also include the ideas of the missing member. This reply keeps you out of a potential discussion on the missing member as the centerpiece of the diversity issue within the company. Sure, that peer group member might be the only female, but that in and of itself is not a reason to postpone discussion on the overall issue at hand. The issue is bigger than any one person or any one perspective. Getting dragged into a discussion about this one individual carries some controversial risk, so avoiding further comment on it is the best way to proceed. Stay focused on the issue and not on any one individual.

Controversy is everywhere around us in our personal and business lives, and it is important to recognize it for what it is, and to take steps to avoid it as often as you possibly can. Getting dragged into controversial discussions is fraught with dangerous consequences, and you will do yourself no favors by allowing yourself to get taken advantage of by others who would seek to wreak havoc on your career by exposing any prejudices that you might have.

FIGURE OUT THE KNOWLEDGE DYNAMICS OF THE ATTENDEES

When you attend a meeting of any kind while at work you will undoubtedly encounter a variety of personality types, experience types, aspiration types, and knowledge types. Personalities will differ widely, as will experience types. Some of the attendees may have many years of experience, while others may have just begun their very first job. Aspirations will differ as well, with some people wanting to someday own a company of their own, while others may be content to work for someone else their entire life. The knowledge factor is one that you will want to penetrate as quickly as you can when attending any meeting. The people with the most knowledge will usually be the ones who speak out the most. People with very little knowledge, perhaps because they are new to the company or new to a particular role, will usually speak out the least. This is because the more knowledgeable people are more comfortable in their environment and more confidant of their own sense of knowing the ins and outs of the company and the subject matter.

Should you find yourself as someone with little knowledge, you then have the opportunity and obligation to become better informed. Maybe you know too little about the company, or you know too little about the meeting topic. Either way you have a chance to learn more about everything that goes on in your company. How will you do this you might be asking? First, you can read up on everything you can find about the company. Start with newsletters, and website news articles, and media articles, and other people within the company, especially the more tenured employees. Second, you can talk directly to the owner or your boss about the history and culture of the company. Third, you can ask questions of other peers, although this can be dicey depending upon the nature of your relationship with a particular peer, or what type of peer member you're talking to (as in one who may be apt to take advantage of you).

If you have too little knowledge related to subject matter expertise, you can begin to do research at the library, or online, or by asking internal subject matter experts for their help. In general people like being asked for their help because it makes them feel important and needed. However there are some people who will use this kind of knowledge imparting opportunity to take advantage of you and your lack of knowledge. This kind of person may feed you incorrect information, or steer you in a direction that may backfire on you at an inopportune time, like during a meeting with the owner. People can be devious, so be on the lookout for those who have knowledge but are also scarce to share it for fear of losing their stature within the company.

Then there are knowledge brokers who will use their expertise to take control over every situation or project that they can get away with, including meetings. These people have no shame about being bossy and arrogant, including talking over the meeting leader or boss or owner. They begin to think that they are the owner or top leader of the company and that they can use their knowledge as a wedge against other peers and maybe even the owner or manager. They might start to think that they couldn't possibly be fired because they know too much and the owner or manager knows too little. This can be especially true in today's business world due to technology.

As an example let's take a company that has been in business for many years and the original founder and owner is now getting older in years. This owner has most likely not had the technology training that younger members of the organization have had over the years. This owner does not have the aptitude for technology related information sharing or website building or computerization of the business. So what do they do? They hire an expert, perhaps someone who has a degree in some technology related field of study, and who has worked in this same field in other companies. Let's say that this new hire has a tremendous amount of knowledge, more than anyone else in the organization by far, and they begin to take undue advantage of their knowledge. They even begin to usurp power and influence from the owner, perhaps to the degree of hiding or inflating certain types of information that are a necessity to the success of the company. They are in essence putting themselves on a pedestal of importance to employees, customers, lenders and the owner. You think this can't happen? Think again, because I have seen it happen with my own eyes at a previous employer.

Knowledge is power; remember that phrase as you go through your working life. Figure out early on who has it and who doesn't in your company, and then do whatever is necessary to enlarge your own knowledge base in order to optimize your career opportunities.

FIGURE OUT OWNER / EMPLOYEE RELATIONSHIPS

If you happen to be in a meeting with a bunch of other employees and the owner or manager is either leading the meeting or is just present in the meeting, you will want to determine which employees, if any, have a closer than normal relationship with the leader. These are the employees who will have a stronger position of influence in the company, and during meetings like the one you are in. There are a variety of factors that go into the closeness of a relationship between owner or manager and employees.

One factor may be the fact that the owner or manager actually hired a particular employee. Another factor might be the knowledge based relationship that we addressed in the last subchapter, where the owner or manager feels that they can't do without a particular employee. Another factor might be an outside of work relationship that is social in nature. Yet another factor may be an outside of work personal relationship that is romantic in nature. Think it can't happen? Think again, as I've seen it happen and more than once. Any of these issues may dictate a closer than typical relationship that shows itself during company meetings. You will see a smile or a wink or a nod or a series of agreements between them that will seem unusual. Try to ascertain which employees are parts of the owner or manager's inner circle, as these are the people who can unduly influence decisions of many types.

I have been part of an inner circle during my working life, and it was primarily because I had been hired by the company owner. It was a relationship built on potential more than on knowledge or personality. Beware of this type of relationship because the owner will eventually and inevitably find someone else, perhaps younger or smarter or more attractive, to focus their attention and admiration on over time. Employee relationships with owners are ripe with the potential for both incredible success opportunities, but also with the potential for being the forgotten golden child. There are owners who seemingly are never satisfied with what they have, and who are always focused on what or who they don't have at any particular point in time.

You will want to figure out who has these relationships so that during meetings you don't inadvertently say something about a particular employee who might very well be part of the owner's inner circle. The owner will be apt to protect their inner circle members because they will normally be those employees who mean the most to the organization or who mean the most on a personal basis. Make the mistake of attacking a member of the inner circle and you will pay the price with being shunned, terminated or banished to a far-away company branch location that no one wants to go to.

You might also see some owner/employee relationships that are not very good. This may be due to employee poor performance but it may also be due to a dissolving personal relationship where a particular employee is on the precipice of being removed for the owner's inner circle. I have also been the receiving end of this conundrum of a situation. I don't know if you will recall a comment that I brought to light in an earlier chapter about a particularly successful event that I was involved in years ago with my employer. I wasn't necessarily expecting an overwhelming amount of kudos from the owner, but I was at least expecting some degree of recognition. What I got at the time was a token mention of admiration for the success, followed by a shot across my bow. The message was this - "That was a great victory, Jim, but that's history now. What have you done for me lately?" Wow, I thought to myself at the time. I just got whacked upside the head verbally for doing a good job. I noted that this kind of event would probably not be the last time it would occur; and in fact it was not. For this owner, nothing was ever good enough. There was always the expectation for more, and the relationship eventually and unfortunately soured over time.

The point is that employee relationships with owners or bosses are something to be wary of and to pay attention to in meetings. Don't make the mistake of getting on the wrong side of an owner / employee relationship that is on solid footing. When you see this kind of relationship you will need to treat it with kid gloves until the relationship falls apart on its own without any help or hindrance from you. Get in the middle of a positive relationship and you are apt to be doomed.

JAMES W. BENDER

WHEN TO VOLUNTEER FOR PROJECTS

Inevitably there will be a number of meetings you attend where the end result will not be a finalized outcome, but more of a project oriented outcome. The leader of the meeting, which could be your boss or even the owner of the company, will ask for volunteers to work on a specific project that is designed to help the company solve a particular problem or issue. In some cases there might not be enough volunteers, in which case the leader will assign some or all of the attendees to the project.

So the question here for you is this - when and why do you volunteer to participate in a project? The easy answer and one that a lot of people would espouse to is this - all the time. These people would say that anytime you can get yourself involved with projects is a way to put yourself forward in the company and get noticed by the boss or owner. That may be true in some cases, but certainly not in all cases. The time to get noticed by the right people and in the right manner is with projects that have a defined and positive outcome that will have a significant impact on the company. Not every project will have the same level of importance and the ones that have less importance may or may not be worth your time and investment.

If you are relatively new to the company then I might suggest that you do in fact volunteer for some of the not-so-important projects so that you can get your feet wet and gain a deeper understanding of project work in general, and how projects can influence company success or failure. If you are more of a tenured employee then you might want to sit on some of the lesser projects, and wait for those opportunities that have the potential of creating a more meaningful outcome for the company. These more meaningful projects can have a bigger impact on your personal notoriety within the company and therefore can have a bigger impact on your career within the company.

Volunteering for a project can have a more beneficial outcome if the other people on the project team are employees that you like and respect. The same holds true for whomever the project leader is that is assigned to the issue. On the other hand if the employees that are on the project team are people that you do not like or who you do not along well with, then your time on the project will not be well spent. The same holds true for a project leader that you are not fond of or someone that you do not work well with as evidenced by something in your past history with that person.

The bottom line here is that picking and choosing your spots on project work is important, and you should take the time to dissect the nature of the project and the people who will be working on that project. Obviously if you are able to volunteer to actually lead a project then by all means go for it. But even in that case be careful to analyze the type of project and the potential for a positive versus negative outcome before you volunteer to be the team leader. Should you mistakenly volunteer to lead a project that ends up with a negative outcome as viewed by your boss or the owner, then you have probably done yourself more harm than good.

Once you have the chance to be a project leader then make sure you take that role seriously. Sure, you will have other employees on the team who will also want to gain some positive exposure from the project outcome, and you will need to allow everyone to have an equal amount of time and input. That said you will also need to make sure that you maintain a degree of control over the project, the agenda, and the other volunteers. You will need to have your own meetings that deal with the project specifics and with only the project team present. You need to have an agenda for every meeting and you need to have a time frame for dialogue, probably no more than one hour, because everyone also has their own job to do as well. If you sense some internal friction during the meetings then you will need to take appropriate steps to counter that friction, inclusive of kicking certain individuals off the project team if necessary to maintain the project timetable and outcome. Project work can be extremely beneficial to you and to the company, but again, be judicious in your choices along the way.

THE MEETING IS OVER - NOW WHAT?

First, let's talk about what you should have been doing during the meeting - taking notes where and when it was most important to do so. Meetings can be long and they can be short in time frame, and they can be deep in material presented and consequence, or they can be short in detail and importance. Meetings that are longer and more detailed in the flow of information are the ones where you will always want to take copious notes. You can't remember every detail of what was said or who presented the materials. Making sure that you have a written memory bank is important in terms of your follow up to every meeting that you attend.

Okay, so now the meeting is over. What are your options in terms of next steps? One option is to do absolutely nothing. Another option is to send a personal note or email to the meeting leader to thank them for their time and efforts, or to maybe even do that face to face, which is always more personal in nature. Another option is to send an email to not only the meeting leader but to all of the meeting participants. It's simply a way to say thanks to everyone for their time and tell them how much you enjoyed the time together, and how much you learned. Another option is to send the note to the meeting leader and follow up on one or two salient points that were discussed at the meeting. Perhaps you can use this email to ask the leader to keep you in mind for future projects and meetings. You can use this post meeting note to create some additional relationship building with the meeting leader and with all of the meeting participants.

The real issue to take note of here is to always take the time to *communicate* in some way with the meeting leader and other attendees. It's just good business sense to do so.

CHAPTER NINE
SURVIVING BUSINESS TRIPS

I vividly remember my very first business trip. I was working in a sales management role and had recently relocated to the east coast. I wasn't on the job very long before the owner of the company announced that a corporate sales meeting would take place in Las Vegas. Of course everyone in the company was quite excited to hear that Las Vegas, sin city as it's called at times by many, was the venue of choice. I recall that many of the salespeople, who all worked under me, all men at the time, were openly talking about having loads of fun at bars and strip clubs. I cautioned all of them as a group and even individually that shenanigans of any kind were likely to backfire on them and me in a large way. I told them to behave themselves and to be professional. You will be the face of our company while there, I had told them.

For whatever reason, and one that everyone regretted later, the company selected travel agent booked all nine of our branch sales staff and me on the same flight to Las Vegas. Several of the salespeople were sitting together on the plane and they evidently were drinking far too much prior to boarding and then again when on the plane. Several of the salespeople who were drinking too much had unwisely decided to throw caution to the wind and continued to drink more and more. There was no stopping them.

Early that same evening during the event, I noticed several of these salespeople slurring their words. I then noticed the owner and spouse move towards this small group of three salespeople, I think more so to just say hello than to critique their intoxication. One of the members of this group shook hands with the owner and spouse, and then proceeded to blurt out something along the lines of telling the spouse that they were older than he had thought and then suggesting to the owner that he could certainly find someone younger and better looking at one of the many Vegas strip clubs, further suggesting that he could go out with him and his buddies later that night to find one.

The owner and spouse walked away, found my boss who was the overall manager of my branch location, and told them that this certain salesperson was to be immediately removed from the event and flown back home as soon as possible, and oh by the way, he was also to be fired immediately. My boss walked over to me, told me about what had just happened, and proceeded to tell me that it was now my problem to relay the news to my sales rep and to get them out of the event and out of town as soon as possible. In other words it was now my problem to fix.

This event was an eye opener for me as a new manager. I thought that I had done what needed to be done prior to the meeting to impress upon my staff the need and importance to maintain a sense of decorum while at this corporate meeting. My efforts were obviously not sufficient enough to have a successful outcome. Not only did I end up losing a salesperson from my staff, but now I too was under the corporate microscope. The owner was now wondering if they had the right sales management person leading the branch. Even my boss at the time was under a microscope, so they too started to wonder I was the right person for the job.

The moral of the story here is that business trips can be enlightening and fun, with lots of great camaraderie and teamwork. They can also be ripe with things that may be beyond your sphere of control; things that can quickly spin out of control, and not in your favor. This chapter will deal with several of the things to take into consideration prior to attending any out of town business trips. These are the things you will need to think about in order to save yourself and perhaps others who work with you or for you, from a calamitous ending. You would be wise to be on your very best behavior while on any business trip, especially your first one!

SUBSTANTIATE EXPENSES & COMPANY POLICY

During a normal business trip you may be tasked with making your own travel arrangements. In a family owned company this is not an unusual circumstance, as most of them do not have enough travel business to warrant the hiring of an outside travel agency. That said, this can happen in any size company so please pay attention. Your arrangements may include airline travel, hotel accommodations, and car rental to name just a few. They may also include taxi service, bus or train service, subway service, and meal arrangements if you are visiting with a client of the company.

Most companies will not provide you with a company credit card, and so they will either request that you utilize your own personal credit card or provide you with a cash advance to cover some of the expenses. Airlines, hotels, and car rental agencies do not deal in cash for advance reservations, so generally speaking you will be using your own credit card to book the arrangements. The cash advance may cover things like trains, subways, buses, tips and meals, but that's about it. The company will stipulate that they will reimburse you for your travel expenses, provided that you supply them with an accurate and well-documented expense report that outlines every single expense involved with your trip.

Rule number one about trips and expense reporting is this - keep every single receipt regardless of how big or how small. This is your only mechanism to prove on paper what and why you spent the company's money. When it comes time for your reimbursement, if you can't prove the expense, then the company will most likely not reimburse you. Rule number two about trips and expense reporting is this - never turn in receipts for things that have no bearing or relevance to the business rationale for your trip. This means that if you have some free time on your hand while on the trip, the company is not going to reimburse you for the time and money you may have spent at the hotel bar, or for a movie you bought on the hotel television, or for tickets to a ball game or some theater event. Each of those items is personal in nature; decisions that you made on your own, and expenses that you decided to bear on your own behalf. Never put them on your expense report! Rule number three about business trips and expense reporting is this - do not lie or misrepresent the truth. Doing so may very well get you fired.

Companies also have time frames for the completion and filing of your expense report. It is not reasonable for you to complete your report a month after your business trip. It is reasonable to complete and submit your report within one week following your return from the trip. That is the norm and so that is what you should be doing. If your company has a one week stipulation as an example, and you fail to submit your report within that time frame, then the company may decide that it is within its right to not reimburse you at all. So beware the company policy for business trips and business expenses. Do not book a flight in first class if the policy indicates that all flights must be booked in a coach class. This mistake will generally come back to bite you big. Staying in a Ritz Carlton hotel will also get you in hot water unless the company policy allows such a stay. Most do not, so again make sure you read the policy. If there is no policy then you must ask the owner for their recommendations and requirements before you make any reservations.

As I indicated previously, business trips can be fun and rewarding from a career standpoint. That said these trips are ripe with pitfalls for those people who decide to take shortcuts or to abuse the company policy. I have personally seen these pitfalls take place, so trust me when I say to you that discretion and good behavior are paramount to a successful trip.

SPENDING THEIR MONEY

No one likes the idea of having other people spend their money. This includes the owner or top management of the company that you work for now or are going to work for in the future. When you are embarking on a business trip for your company, you are also spending the company's money to do so. Your owner or manager will not take kindly to any attempts on your part to spend money in a frivolous fashion. Earlier in this chapter I mentioned a couple of those frivolous classifications as flying first class or staying at a Ritz Carlton hotel. Now don't get me wrong, I would love to fly first class and stay at Ritz Carlton hotels as often as possible, and maybe the owner of your company actually does both, but the owner does not want you to do what they do. They want you to be economical. They want you to be prudent. They want you to be budget conscious. They want you to spend as little money as possible in order to accomplish your mission for travelling.

This kind of frugality, which by the way I completely understand, can have some adverse consequences for you, the traveler. As an example I once worked for a company where the owner made all travel plans for employees who were going on business trips. The airport that this owner chose for air travel was a three hour drive from my home, while there was another airport that was just one hour from my home. When I inquired about changing airports based on my travel time, the response I received was a resounding no. The airport further away had cheaper flights, so that's the way it was going to be. This choice was great for the owner but quite inconvenient for me. The owner did not care about my issues at all; they only cared about saving money. This was perhaps a very smart policy for the owner to put in place, but perhaps it was also an unnecessary burden for their employees which could lead to a bit of disgruntlement. In fact, after several of these frugality ridden business trips that I endured, I decided that I was working for the wrong company and the wrong type of owner. Good for the owner was bad for me and my primary interest was on me not them.

This was a prime example of perhaps an owner being penny wise and pound foolish. That is not to say that I don't understand where the owner was coming from, but employees also want to work in an environment where their personal time and inconvenience is taken into consideration. This particular owner chose the cost savings route over their employee's personal time and satisfaction level. I can see where people can understand both sides on this type of equation, and you may very well have a scenario where you are put in a similar situation during your employment.

Budget minded owners want you to travel in an inexpensive manner, so choose wisely if your owner or direct manager gives you the ability to plan your own travel arrangements. The bottom line here is this - don't do what you would want to do, just do what you think the owner or manager would want you to do. You want to spend nickels like they are manhole covers. Hang on to your nickels and dimes, and spend as little as possible in order to get your job done. This is especially true for your first business trip and during your first year on the job.

WATCH OUT FOR THE PARTY PEOPLE

Again, during your first business trip and even those that may come afterwards, you want to be extremely mindful of everything and everyone that you encounter. There will be that certain set of employees who see their business trip as a means to let loose, and to do so on the company's money. When you see these people run the other direction. I said run, not walk, because the people that make up this kind of crowd will get you in hot water with the owner or company leader more often than not. They are troublemakers and not to be trusted at any time. How will you know who they are you might be asking?

You will know when you see the same people gathering together and whispering to one another in hushed voices. They are usually a small group of employees who know one another well, and who have gone off the deep end together more than once. They are reluctant to ask anyone else to join their group because they don't know who they can and cannot trust. They talk in a quiet tone so no one hears what they are up to.

You may find yourself being asked to join them one day. If and when they do, then you will need to decide how to respond. Will it be the ringleader who asks you or will it be one of the other members of the party group? If you are a relatively new employee and worse yet if this would be your first business trip, you will need to be extremely careful with your response. The last thing you want to do is get in unforeseen situations when you are a new employee, and at the same time you don't want to be seen by your peers as an outsider. You want to have predetermined excuses ready to go when and if you get an invite, so think about what those excuses will be ahead of time. Rehearse them in your head several times over so that you will be ready with a reply almost instantaneously. The quicker you respond to an invitation the more credible your response will sound. Stand there and stall while thinking of an excuse will be seen as just that - you will be seen as an outsider and you will probably be treated as one long after this episode.

What are some good excuses to use? Well, you can always say that you're not feeling well and you need to get some additional rest. You can say that you promised your kids that you would call them at a certain time that same evening. If you say you need to call your spouse you may get mocked by others, but calling your kids is a whole different matter. You can say that you already made other plans, but maybe next time. That's a good one because you're keeping the door open for another invitation at a later date, time and place. Telling people that you need to read up on tomorrow's meeting agenda will sound standoffish. You're basically telling them that should be doing the very same thing that you plan on doing, and that will not sit well with the party group.

What kind of trouble could you foresee happening with a party animal group of fellow employees? The list is probably endless, but here are a few of the more predictable outcomes. You end up at a strip club and the night gets far worse after you arrive due to excessive drinking and carousing. Fights are known to break out at these clubs, especially late at night. You end up drinking all night with a bunch of guzzlers who have done this far too many times, and you either pass out at the bar or are so hung over that you miss the entire next day of meetings. This will not sit well with your boss or the top manager of the company. You end up in jail after being charged with public intoxication, public urination, or fighting. None of these are good outcomes. Remember the salesperson that I mentioned earlier who drank too much and said all the wrong things to the owner's spouse during the first night's opening festivities?

I recall someone, I think it was a minister giving a Sunday sermon years ago, who said something that stuck with me form many years. They were talking about human behavior habits and how those habits manage to sometimes put people in situations that they later regret. The minister said something along the lines of this - be careful who you choose as friends or who you choose to hang out with, because you are very likely to end being up being someone more like them than who you were before you met them. What the minister was saying was that if you choose to hang with the wrong crowd, then you will probably end up being a member of the wrong crowd. That is not where you want to end up; trust me on that one.

Be smart, be alert, be careful, and be judicious with your time and your body. Make the wrong choices and you are likely to pay dearly for them down the road. Make the right choices and your career will be the better for it.

EATING AND DRINKING HABITS

Everybody likes to eat and have fun, and everybody likes to have an occasional cocktail, beer or glass of wine. However there is a limit to everything, and I would encourage you to pay close attention to this while on company business trips. Believe it or not, the habits you display while on business trips can make or break one's career path. If you display poor habits while eating and drinking, then you are at risk for being ostracized by your peers, your boss and your company leader. You may even have issues with company clientele if you display poor habits while dining with them. What kind of habits am I talking about here?

Let's start with your dining habits. Do you know what fork or spoon to use if you're dining out at one of the finer restaurants? You have no doubt sat down at an expensive restaurant for dinner one day and observed a tableware array of spoons, forks and knives that made you wonder what in the world they were all used for. I certainly have had that happen to me in the past. So what did I do? First, I waited to do much of anything until I saw what other diners did with their array of tableware. Behold the powers of observation because you can learn a lot by watching others. Once I saw how others handled things I proceeded on my own. Second, the next day I went online to research the appropriate manners to use when faced with dining out at a higher priced and more elegant restaurant. By doing this research I gave myself an opportunity to learn the ropes and memorize the best way to handle this kind of situation in the future.

Another thing to pay attention to are your table manners while eating. People will be watching your every move. Moves you say; what moves? Will you be putting too much food in your mouth at one time? Will you have food coming out of your mouth, dribbling down your chin? Will you be talking with food in your mouth? Will you be holding your fork in an appropriate manner while eating? Will you be slurping your drink and making all sorts of weird noises while swallowing? Will you be talking with drink in your mouth? Maybe you're laughing while reading this and wondering how people could do any of these things. Well trust me when I say that I've seen people do these things and a lot more during my many years of travelling on business trips. Make sure you read up on what good manners are before you do on your first trip, and then pay close attention to how others behave while eating.

If you're a wine drinker then I would hope that you know how to hold a glass in the appropriate manner. Make sure you do some research to make sure that you do know how to hold a glass while dining with peers, your boss or the owner of your company. There is a right way and there is a wring way to do this, I kid you not. The same thing can be said for drinking a beer. Let's say you order a bottle of beer for lunch or dinner while dining with a client. Your server inquires whether you want a glass with your bottle of beer. The correct response is to say yes. Miss Manners says that drinking your beer out of the bottle would not be an appropriate way to imbibe your beverage of choice while dining. Sure, it's fine if you're out with your friends at a local pub, but it's not okay if you're on a business trip and you are having dinner with a client or with your boss or owner. Use good manners when you're out and your career will be helped by doing so.

GOING TO BED

I know, I know, now you're thinking that I'm about to tell you when and how to go to bed much like your mother would have done umpteen years ago when you were probably acting like a brat at times. No, I'm not going to tell you when to go to bed but I am going to suggest when you should go to bed. Why would I do this and why is it so important?

Remember that while on a business trip you are representing your company and your owner or boss. You are the face of the company that employs you, and others will be looking at you with hawk-like eyes. Part of being a company representative is presenting yourself in the most positive light possible, which means you need to get a good night's sleep so that you are rested and fresh to face the next days' activities. Go to bed too late and you might wake up with dark circles or bags under your eyes. Go to bed inebriated and the effect will be worse. Eat the wrong food during the evening and you may wake up with the runs or worse. Paying attention to these types of details is extremely important in order that you put your best foot forward at all times during your business trip.

One of the simplest ways to ensure that you get the rest you need is to set a timetable for when you make the decision to retire for the evening, go back to your hotel room and go to bed. Maybe you're one of these people who don't normally need a lot of sleep, and you're used to going to bed at midnight or even later. That may work for you at home, but keep in mind that hardly anyone sleeps as well on the road while in a hotel than they do at home in their own bed. Don't make the mistake of thinking that you will sleep as well as you normally do because it is very likely that you will not do so. Business travel and all of the activities related to that travel will take a toll on almost everyone. Hotel rooms are generally not as quiet as maybe you're used to at home. Hotel lobbies and hallways are full of people coming and going, people have their televisions on too loud, guests are making too much noise in their room next to yours, and a host of other issues that you don't encounter at home. All of these nuisances may affect your sleep pattern, so setting a time for getting into bed will be important in order to minimize the impacts of sleeping in hotel rooms.

Another important point here is to make sure that you go to bed alone while on business trips. I am hoping that you know exactly what I mean here! Hooking up with someone while on a business trip is just plain bad news. It may seem satisfying for a period of time, but inevitably your rendezvous will come back to haunt you. You may end up with everyone in your company finding out about your tryst. You may end up with some kind of sexually transmitted disease. That should be fun to explain to your life partner when you get home. You may end up oversleeping and miss an important meeting or appointment. You may end up hooking up with someone who has a wife or husband back home and if so, how will you feel about being part of a future marital breakup? Someone may see you or your sleeping partner sneaking out of the hotel room the next morning and video the departure. Maybe you will end up on YouTube by days end. Maybe there's a camera in your room and the entire night's events have been captured on film for future blackmailing attempts by some sinister group. The list of bad news possibilities is almost endless, so why take the chance to do it? Just behave yourself and go to bed at a reasonable hour and alone.

ALL EYES ARE WATCHING YOU

Your first business trip in particular will be one where nearly everyone else in your travel contingent will be casting a wondering eye toward you, and they will be doing so at all times. Some of them will be looking for any slight misstep so they can report their findings back to higher authorities in the company. These are the people who are not your friends. They are not the ones who will not have your back when the chips are down. These are the people who love to gossip and they love to spread rumors, especially those that will suit their own purposes for eliminating some of their internal competition. If you have a tendency to stray from some of the aforementioned guidelines that I mentioned, they will be right there to catch you in the act. They will relish the opportunity to throw you under the bus as often as possible.

Imagine being at an aquarium and looking through the glass to see the array of fish or sharks or manatee or porpoise. I personally love going to the aquarium and walking around to witness a variety of nature's most unique creatures of the sea, lakes and rivers. You are as close to a shark as you will probably ever be, and you feel safe from any possibility of something bad happening. You are a spectator and you love seeing, because seeing this for real is enables you to believe, especially when it comes to looking up close at a shark. You marvel at the complexities of this wondrous opportunity to gain the proximity that you have to witness a killer of the oceans, or at least that's what the *Jaws* movies would have us believe.

A SURVIVAL GUIDE ON WORKING FOR A FAMILY OWNED COMPANY

Now let's turn the tables and make you the one that is inside a glass enclosed area. Now you are the one on display, and everyone walking around is looking at you. They are studying your every move and your every habit. They are looking for something to go wrong, because after all, that's what they like to see the most - human failure is at the heart of most people. They relish seeing people fail or to have difficulties. They want to know that others have faults of their own, just like they do. They want to make themselves more human by seeing you put to the test, perhaps a test that they have already undergone in the past. They are watching you and hoping they can see something that they can report back to the owner, something that will make you look bad so that they can look better.

People will be watching you at breakfast, at lunch, at dinner, and during any and all meetings of any type. They are not looking at you in awe to see your many talents. They are looking at you to find a chink in your armor, a little nugget of your personal misfortune that they can use for their benefit. So what do you do? How can you best handle this type of daunting situation, knowing that others are constantly watching your every move?

The best advice I can give you is to always be wary and to always beware. You are on candid camera so you need to always know that others are watching. Always think in advance and always act responsibly at every occasion. Never turn a blind eye thinking that no one is around you to see what you are doing or what you are saying. That would be a very naïve way of thinking on your part. You may think no one is watching, but believe me, they are watching your every move. You are in a fish bowl so follow my advice and always be on your very best behavior.

TIMELINESS

Business trips are generally laced with precision oriented time schedules. Meetings are prearranged and set in stone. Whatever the reason for the out of town trip, people expect you to be on time, every time, regardless of the circumstances. Maybe your trip centers on a meeting with clients, or maybe it revolves around s company arranged meeting that is designed as educational or supportive. Again, regardless of the nature of the trip, you will be expected to arrive for any and all events on time. What does on time mean to you?

On time means being present at whatever event is may be earlier than the start time. If the event start time is 8 a.m. then you will need to be there by 7:55 a.m. That is what on time means to me if I'm the one showing up for a meeting or some other form of event. It does not mean 8:01 a.m., because that would mean you are late. Being late is never acceptable, regardless of reason. It is your responsibility to make whatever accommodations necessary in order to arrive early for your meetings and other events.

Other timing oriented issues on your business trip include showing up on time for your flight, if you have one, as well as any other travel related itinerary items that you may have to rely on in order to get to where you need to be. Travel can be difficult at times and you will need to be aware of the myriad of delays and interruptions that can occur at any time at any place. You cannot do much to overcome the delays and interruptions that are beyond your control, but you can plan your travel itinerary to minimize these types of events. If you need to be present at an event at 8 a.m., then try not to arrange a flight that departs late at night. Instead book a flight that departs late morning or early afternoon to minimize any impact of potential delays or cancellations. This is what I mean by controlling your own destiny to whatever degree possible.

I don't really have a lot more to add to the issue of timeliness. The importance is self-evident and the means to achieve the necessary objective are pretty basic in nature. As the Nike ad says, *just do it*! You are in complete control so make it happen.

REMEMBER THAT EVERYONE HAS A PHONE WITH A CAMERA

Remember the aquarium story from a previous subchapter? Everyone is always watching you because you're in a bubble, right? Well, these days everyone has a phone and every phone has a camera to capture every event imaginable. It seems as though no matter where you are, who you're with, or what you're doing you are under constant surveillance by people armed with cell phone cameras. You have undoubtedly seen numerous tapes of footage from cell phones on the evening news, where people capture accidents, crimes, and other video that the perpetrators wish no one had seen. This kind of scenario is reminiscent of the old television show *Candid Camera* hosted by Allen Funk. The show captured unsuspecting people on film who were doing things that they would later regret by virtue of people laughing at their turn of events.

Sure, this show resulted in things happening to people that were funny. In your role as an employee on a business trip however, you are far more likely to have someone capturing you doing something that might not be so funny. Maybe someone takes film of you picking your nose; well sure, that might be seen as funny by some people, but your peers or your boss or the owner might not find it quite as funny as others, especially if you were in a discussion with a client. Maybe someone captures you scratching your crotch or your butt in a most fervent manner. That's going to look good on YouTube, right? So how do you guard against being the object of someone's camera ready cell phone?

Start by paying close attention to everything you are doing. Recognize that people are looking at you and waiting for an opportunity to catch you doing something unconventional; something that would be worthy of showing others on either YouTube or Facebook or some other sharing mechanism. You do not want to be the butt of someone's idea of a joke, and most likely the person taking the shot won't even be someone you know. So be very careful how you conduct yourself, and be very wary of who else is around you that might be able to capture your every move and word. You will be glad that you did so.

CHAPTER TEN
SURVIVING YOUR PROMOTION

Congratulations! You have managed to both stay out of trouble and do a stellar job at whatever position you have held with the company, and by succeeding at both you have found yourself being promoted to a new job with a new title and new responsibilities. Hopefully your promotion also comes with a significant increase in salary, incentives and benefits. If not, you have my sympathy, as you are evidently employed by a scrooge who takes undue advantage of people who work for their company.

What you need to recognize is that the majority of promotions come with a significant difference in your level of responsibilities with regard to productivity and people skills. People who get promotions are expected to do more for their employer. They are expected to work longer hours, travel when requested to do so, hire and fire people, produce better quality results and higher profit margins, and to always show loyalty to their boss and company owner. There is good news and bad news that come with promotions, so make sure you give due thought to the specifics of your promotion before you accept the new job and the new responsibilities that come with that new job.

Management is far different than being a regular employee. For one thing your success may very well depend on how well the employees who work for you succeed at their individual jobs. Your success will no longer be singular in nature, meaning that it in the past your success was due in large part by your own personal work habits and achievements. Now with your new role your success will be multidimensional, meaning that your employees may very well control the outcome of your new job responsibilities. Are you ready for that kind of role? Do you realize how different that role is compared to your last job? Do you recognize that management means that more eyes are looking at your everyday performance and judging your every move? Is that the kind of job, exposure and stress that you want?

This chapter is dedicated to enlightening you on the many changes and differences that come with promotions. Many of the changes are quite positive. Some will be not so positive and thereby create some challenges that you may not be aware of. I will help point out some ways that you can ensure your own success and continue to move up the ladder.

ONE STEP CLOSER TO THE TOP

Promotions generally mean that you are now one step closer to the top job in the company. A promotion does in fact mean that you are moving up the managerial ladder, regardless of the type of company you might work for. If you recall the chapter that explained what organizational charts mean to a company's hierarchal structure then you know that your promotion moves you upward on the chart. That means that you are closer to the top rung on the chart than you were previously.

However, you may also recall the chapter where I explained that family owned companies tend to be managed at the top levels by family members of the original owner. If this is indeed the case with the company that you work for, then you are clearly moving up the organizational ladder and getting closer to the top, but it also means that you most likely have very little chance for becoming the top person in the company. You are not family related so that means you will have a certain point in time at your current employer where your ability to achieve a higher rung will cease to exist. At that point you either need to recognize that scenario for what it is and accept that fact, or make the decision to move on and find a new employer. Each of those situations is fine from my perspective; it will simply depend on your own levels of tolerance and ambition as to what kind of choice you make at that time in your career.

Being one step closer to the top also means that you now have an entirely new set of peers to work with and to worry about. Your peers before you got a promotion were basically all lower level, but same level peers. We will assume that none of them, or you, had any managerial responsibility in that job classification. Now you have jumped up the organization chart by at least one level, while perhaps none of your prior peers had that happen to them at the same time. Suddenly your place on the organizational chart has brought about a new set of people who are welcoming you to their peer level. Or, are they really welcoming you with open arms or are they just pretending to do so?

Your promotion has conceivably brought about a new set of internal competitors for what they, and maybe you too, see as their next promotion up the ladder. There is no question that people can be very competitive while hoping to gain added attention and added responsibilities. This ambition can be wielded blindly by some, while openly harmonious by others. The people with blind ambition can be untrustworthy, ruthless, deceitful, dishonest, vengeful and manipulative. There may be some peers of yours that fit into this category, and if so you will need to identify them out as quickly as you possibly can. Failure to do so can bring about an enormous amount of unwelcome and unneeded diversions that will all be designed to make you look bad in the eyes of your boss and company owner. These folks will do whatever it takes to get ahead, and if that means throwing you under the bus, then so be it, because they will do so.

Your new peers that are openly harmonious about their competitive nature and their aspirations for more promotions down the road means that they will be far better peers to have some degree of trust in as you work together. But make sure you never forget that even these peers will want to beat you out for the next level job promotion. Business is very much like sports in that individual competitors are involved with both areas. Look at it like you would if you were watching the U.S. Women's Olympic Gymnastics Team. Each of the team members wants to win their individual event, but at the same time they all want to do their very best in the team competition for the benefit of the U.S. squad and their country. This same type of personal dynamic takes place in business, where each peer member wants to be the one chosen for the next promotion, yet they all want to do well and work well together for the overall benefit of the company. Competition is prevalent throughout business, throughout sports, and throughout life in general.

When you start getting promotions other people in your company start to look at you differently. They may not be as friendly as they used to be, or at least that might be the way you perceive it. Lower level employees have a tendency, whether it is it right or wrong, to have a certain amount of distrust in management personnel. This same kind of distrust takes place in politics as well, where the same public that first voted people into office later exhibit a certain distrust of all politicians. I believe that both scenarios are inherent in their respective situations and therefore need to be recognized with a certain degree of normalcy rather than seeing them as unique. If you take the approach that a certain amount of distrust is to be expected you can then move forward knowing that you need to always keep that in mind as you begin your new promotion. If people start to treat you differently you can accept that as more of the norm than a personal slight.

There are indeed many good things about getting promoted and there are many bad things as well. In the next few subchapters we will take a closer look at both the good and the bad.

THE GOOD NEWS

There is an abundance of good news that is readily apparent when you get promoted to a new job classification. For example, you will undoubtedly (I hope and presume) be receiving an increase in salary, a bonus or incentive compensation structure that allows you to earn more based on your personal performance as well as your company's performance, and even an enhanced benefit package that provides better insurance coverages for you and your family. Perhaps you will even receive a monthly automobile allowance or club membership privileges or stock options/company ownership shares (although this is more unlikely to take place in family owned companies).

More good news includes things like better parking spaces (which I personally do not like nor endorse), train or subway passes that are fully paid for by the company, a company credit card that can be used for business travel and entertainment, a gas card for your automobile if you receive an auto allowance, a nicer office or bigger office or one with windows, and of course the new opportunity you now have to interact more closely with the company ownership or leadership.

You are now a member of the company's internal management club, someone who is looked at differently and perhaps even looked up to by lower level employees. Maybe you will like this newfound notoriety that comes with a position of authority, or maybe you will shy away from it. Maybe you will like the increased scrutiny that comes with authority and responsibility, or maybe you will wish that you could just do your job without having more eyes on you all of the time. I can tell you that most people who have the opportunity to become part of management enjoy their newfound celebrity status inside the company. They love the attention and they love the benefits that come with the attention.

Management is not all good news however, and there are some people who later wish that they had not been promoted.

THE BAD NEWS

Increased responsibility and authority can, for some people, be an albatross around their neck. This can occur for many reasons. One is that some people will not like the increased scrutiny and stress levels that come with being promoted. Another is that some people will abuse their new authority and become bullies inside their workplace. Yet another is that some people will not be adequately prepared or experienced for their new job role, and yet another is that some people will just plain suck at being managers. Management is far different from being a lower level worker.

I have seen some people who were promoted for all the wrong reasons. Some received their promotion by virtue of a friendship or close relationship with their direct supervisor or the owner. These people were not the best choice for the open managerial position, but the owner or boss knew that the person they chose would be loyal to them after the promotion took effect. In this kind of case where the best candidate did not get the job, the company suffers, the other employees suffer, and the candidate passed over suffers. Company owners and managers are not perfect and they do make bad decisions from time to time. You then, as an employee, have every right to make a decision to either remain working in this environment or to leave and find a different arena.

Some people get promoted by virtue of having the ability or situation by which they can or are holding something over the head of the promoting employee (which may be the owner or top manager). I have seen situations in the past where let's say an owner's kid gets into a particularly bad mess; let's say by drinking too much while with other employees or by getting into legal trouble and one of the other employees knowing about it, or by engaging in sexual harassment. Employees who have seen an owner or owner's kid involved in a potentially compromising situation may use their knowledge to blackmail their boss in a subtle manner, insinuating that a promotion might serve them both well in the future. This would be an example of someone who got promoted for the wrong reason from a business perspective, but for perhaps a good reason from an owner's personal perspective.

Bad promotions are like bad hires. They are basically harmful to the company and to the internal culture of the company. They end up creating far more harm than good. A bad promotion can wear on the employees that report to this person. Maybe the better candidate now reports to this person and they leave the company knowing they were the better choice but were overlooked. Maybe the other employees that now report to this person have no respect for them, and therefore the department involved becomes dysfunctional, out of control, and painfully detrimental to the stability of the company as a whole.

Managing people is vastly different from simply doing your own job. We will take a look at why that is the case.

MANAGEMENT IS DIFFERENT

Let's use an example here and say that you are working at a local beauty salon as a hair stylist. Your boss is the owner of the company and the company has been performing well financially over the two years that you have been employed there. You have also done a good job by not only performing your own job well but by also bringing in new clients. Your boss, the owner of the salon, likes you. You work a regular schedule of five days per week, Tuesday through Saturday, from 9 a.m. - 4 p.m. every day. You are married and have children who attend school. You enjoy where you work and you enjoy the camaraderie that you have with the other stylists and personnel that work at the salon.

One day the owner of the salon asks to meet with you after hours for a quick drink at the tavern nearby. The owner wants to discuss an upcoming change that will take place. You are curious and so you agree to meet. At that meeting the owner informs you that they are opening a new salon on the other side of town, and they want you to be the manager of this new enterprise. The job comes with a base salary that is significantly higher than what you were being paid, plus a percentage of the salon's profits at the end of the year. You are immediately ecstatic because you have been promoted. You have been a star performer and now you are getting your just reward. You tell the owner on the spot that you will take the job. Now what?

After further discussions with the owner you begin to realize that management will be different. For starters, you are expected to recruit, hire and train an entirely new staff of stylists and accompanying staff members. In addition you are expected to be onsite at the new salon every day and during all hours that they are open. The hours are from 9 a.m. to 7 p.m., Tuesday through Friday, and 9 a.m. to 3 p.m. on Saturday. The hours are considerably different than your previous work hours. Next, since you are the manager you are also expected to be the person opening the doors in the morning and relocking them after closing (after the last client and all staff leave). This means that you will be starting at 8:30 a.m. on your work days and probably not leaving until 7:30 p.m. on weekdays and 3:30 p.m. on Saturdays. Suddenly you are starting to get a headache just thinking about the workload. But wait - there's more!

You have not discussed this promotion with your spouse and have perhaps not thought through the many implications involved with your children. Furthermore this new salon on the other side of town is a solid forty minute drive from home compared to the seven minute drive to your current place of employment. So your time spent away from home just got longer by almost an hour per day just by virtue of the driving. Your time went up as did your projected cost of fuel and wear and tear on your car. All of a sudden you begin to realize that this new job is going to entail a lot more out of you than you first thought.

So, you finally realize the many time constraints and expectations that this new promotion requires, and now comes the much harder part of recruiting competent and reliable employees, retaining these employees, teaching these employees, managing these employees, keeping time charts, doing payroll, dealing with all of the clients, and ad infinitum. The job is enormous in time and complexities compared to your previous job. Now you may want to take a step back and make a more educated and informed determination of just how much you really want this promotion.

I have had a mantra of sorts over my many years of management - management wouldn't be so bad if it weren't for people. How's that for some sticker shock! The mantra means that the main problem with the job of management is people, the very employees that report to you. People are the main problem because they themselves are full of problems, some personal and some professional, and they seemingly find a myriad of ways to pass their problems on to you and make them your problems. People have all sorts of excuses they come up with to miss work, show up late for work, forget to do the work, be late with the work, be incomplete with the work, fail to understand the work, etc., etc. I think you get the main point by now.

Management is a lot harder than you might think, and it's not for everyone. Maybe it's not for you. Maybe it is for you. Either way the only way to really find out is to give it a try. Then you get to make your own decision and move forward as you see fit.

SUCCESS IS NO LONGER SINGULAR

Before you got promoted you were one of the lower level employees and most of your success was derived by virtue of your own performance on the job. Your success was singular in nature, meaning that it was purely your own efforts that determined your success or failure. No one else helped you do it for the most part, and you did not have to depend on others around you in order for your boss to determine your overall job performance.

Now that you received your promotion, gauging your success has become an entirely different picture. Sure, you do have some personal responsibilities that may come with your new job, but for the most part your success will depend on how others perform at their individual and collective jobs. If they fail, you fail. If they succeed, you succeed. Your success is no longer singular in nature, but rather quite multifaceted. How do you like the sound of that? Remember the recent story above the stylist that got promoted to manager of a new location? How do you think that person is going to be judged in terms of success? Their success will be partially determined by the success of all of the other employees. Will there be enough good employees? Will the good employees stay with the company? Will the location make any money, because financial success will come from having enough good, competent employees who stay with the job on a longer term basis? Yeah, I think you're starting to see the pattern here of success through others. That's what management is. Welcome to the real world of management my friends!

Since your success now depends on others, what do you do if your employees stage a revolt, or fail to show up for work, or if one of them is a troublemaker? What do you do if one of them causes a serious problem with one of your best clients? Hey, you're the manager now, so all of the decisions that need to be made are yours to decide and implement. How does management sound now? Still think you want to be in management and continue to climb the corporate ladder? Read on and you will have more to think about.

FIGURE OUT WHO AND WHAT YOU HAVE WORKING FOR YOU

After your promotion takes place, one of the first things you will need to do as a new manager is to take the temperature, so-to-speak, of your staff. Who are they, how many of them are there, what do they do, what are their strong points, what are their weak points, and will they fit into your own game plan? Remember, your success is now going to depend more and more on those people who work for you, so making sure you are sufficiently up to speed on your team is critical.

The "who" part of your direct report team, and maybe even some people under your directs, takes some time because you will need to meet with each individual and do two things - ask questions and listen for clues. A one on one meeting is your best way to get to know your team as individuals and as members of your team. You want to know something about them personally and professionally. What you're really digging for are clues for how receptive they will be to your own game plan and not just the last boss they worked for. I've seen a lot of good employees pivot into bad ones after their favorite boss left the position. Personal preferences and personal loyalties are sometimes hard to break away from, especially when a new boss steps into the picture. You will want to know for certain that your team will have a sense of loyalty to you and to respect the decisions that you may make in the future.

The next assessment of your team will focus on how good each employee is at their job function. There's the personality side that we've already talked about, but this is the job capability and capacity portion of the job. You will need to determine how well they have historically performed, and you can do that by reading their performance reviews and talking to their past boss and other company leaders. You can also give out various task assignments early in your promotion role to give you an accurate measure of your staff's knowledge and work habits. Trust me when I tell you that you don't really want to take everyone else's advice on your team member capability. You do not want to leave that to chance.

What do you do if you find out that you have a bad apple or two on your team? Can you just arbitrarily get rid of them? Can you just fire them at will and hire who you want? Those are all serious questions that have serious implications and consequences. Generally speaking you cannot decide to arbitrarily get rid of an employee, especially one that has a good deal of tenure with the company. Firing people these days requires that you have a good paper trail of job performance issues and corrective action opportunities. Even though your company may have an at-will employment policy, which means that either they or you can decide to abort the employment role at any time, there are certain statutes, laws, and protocols that bring about the need to have a rational reason for you to fire someone. What does this mean?

It means that if you determine that you have a bad apple, someone who doesn't quite fit your idea of an ideal employee, then you may have to follow internal company policies and guidelines in order to build a logical, rational and legal case for your decision to terminate someone. That's just the way business life works these days. Legal precedents are an important part of employment law and employment practice in almost every kind of company. Your human resources department can help you with this kind of issue, but if your company does not have such a department, then you will need to tread lightly and speak to the company owner or top manager in some detail before proceeding with any termination actions.

Also keep in mind that some of the employees who now work for you may have been hired by the company owner or top leader. That can bring some serious issues for you if you're not keenly aware of an employee's company history. Make sure you know when an employee was hired, who hired them, and if there is some kind of familial or friendship relationship between the owner and the employee. Make the wrong choice at the wrong time without knowing all the details and you could be the one getting shown the exit door. Details are important in management.

DETAILS, DETAILS, DETAILS

You have no doubt heard the phrase "the devil is in the details", right? Well, that is especially true in management. Business in general requires precision timing in just about everything you do. Customers are inclined to make purchases and do business with people and companies that serve their purpose on time, every time. Let's take a look at an example of what I mean here.

Assume that you work at a local automobile dealership. You have worked in the service and repairs department for a couple of years and suddenly the service manager is terminated. The owner comes to you and asks you to take the job. Congratulations, you have just been promoted! Now all of the service technicians report to you. Now your former peers are your direct reports, and they take orders from you. You are no longer their friend, you're their supervisor. You were the best technician the dealership had, and now the best tech is no longer a tech.

It turns out that the service department had been having problems with getting repairs done in a timely fashion. The previous service manager was tasked with fixing the problem, but they failed to do so, at least according to customers. You noticed the issue in the past, but now you have the opportunity, and the responsibility, to get things right. The owner is counting on you to fix the problem. You are now in the position of doing some serious research to determine why the problems occurred, because you can't fix what you don't know or understand. Your research means that you have to be concerned about details rather than thoughts or ideas or assumptions. Knowing the details will help fix the problem.

After your research you discover that the parts manager is part of the problem because repairs are lagging behind an acceptable time frame due to parts not being readily available. It appears the parts manager is being compromised with a local parts supplier by virtue of a family relationship, and the parts manager has neglected to find an alternative source for the parts. Is the problem the parts manager, the parts supplier, both parties, or your previous service department manager, or the owner or manager's decision to not carry very many parts in house? Getting to the root of the problem requires knowing all of the details before deciding how to fix the problem. This is just a simple overview displaying the importance of details in providing service to customers in a timely basis so that they keep coming back to your employer. If they don't come back, then your company suffers a decline in revenue and you might be out of a job.

Details are usually at the root of any problem, but sometimes people can be part of the problem too. In the case of the auto dealership, part of the problem clearly was the service manager and the parts manager. Neither of them reacted or responded quickly enough to determine the cause of customer discontent or to fix the delay problems. So, do you blame the two of them more than the parts supplier or do you now also take a look at the owner of the dealership, because the service manager did report directly to the owner? Managers need to realize that the buck stops with them, something Harry Truman used to say years ago when he was President of the United States. Wherever there is a problem and however it occurred, the top manager in the company has the ultimate accountability for providing quality service to their customers, and fixing any problems. You, as a department manager, have the responsibility of providing the necessary service achievements so that the owner does not have to get involved with fixing the problems. You are expected to hit all of your service and quality targets. That is your job!

HITTING THE TARGETS

Targets in the sense of business jargon, are the objectives that you as a manager have on your plate for the department or business segment that you have responsibility for in the company. These business targets may be based on timing issues, financial issues, sales issues, quality issues, and profit issues. They may also include some soft skill objectives such as employee recruitment and retention, team orientation and your ability to work well with others, direct report ratings of your managerial ability, and visionary thinking.

Objectives are the means by which your boss and/or the owner will measure your job performance. Most companies and supervisors realize that any more than five key objectives are likely to dilute the effectiveness of any attempt to achieve meaningful success. There can be lots of secondary targets or objectives but more than five primary targets puts far too much stress on far too many areas. Regardless of the number of targets that you end up with at your company, it is paramount to achieve the top primary targets that you are given. Hopefully your boss or the owner has asked you for your input on the targets because that would be instrumental in getting you to buy in to your targets. No one likes arbitrary objectives that are handed down from the mountain, so-to-speak, but they do like a set of targets that they had a role in setting.

Management is different from being a lower level employee because you are tasked with achieving results through others, as well as yourself. Managers are required to focus on the bigger picture for sure, but they are also tasked with meeting short term goals and long term goals. Short term goals can be measured in days, weeks, months, quarters and years. Goals can measured in percentages, dollars, margins, earnings, return on equity, and a whole host of other outcomes. Goals can be measured in increases, decreases, trend lines, and forecasts.

The overriding thing to remember is that as a manager you are expected to hit the targets, no questions asked. Are there circumstances that could be beyond your control that end up providing less than satisfactory results? Yes, there are things that happen beyond your control, but you are expected to be a visionary to a degree and project a series of assumptions that could have a negative effect on your hitting all the targets. If you can project outcomes then you should be able to make the necessary adjustments within the scope of your control and authority to remain on track for hitting your targets. That's what great managers do - they think short term and long term and probability outcomes. It's certainly not the same job expectations that you had prior to getting your first promotion.

Hitting the targets is your main job as a manager. Hit five out of five and you are in good shape; hit four out of five and you are on thin ice; hit three out of five and you better react fast or be looking for a new job; hit two out of five and you're history. Management is rarely about what you did yesterday. It's all about what have you done lately. What have you achieved today and what will you achieve tomorrow? Yesterday's successes are like yesterday's newspaper. Old news is already a given. Tell me something I don't already know, that's what management is all about. It is a constant struggle to keep up with new targets, realigned targets, modified targets and additional targets. The stress can be a killer to some who can't handle constant change and ever-increasing expectation levels.

Be prepared to deal with today and tomorrow, and be a visionary in your thinking.

VISIONARY THINKING

Now that you have been promoted into a position of more authority and responsibility, you are also expected to be a voice of the future. You are now expected to be thinking not only about yesterday's results and today's results, but also about the future of the enterprise in general. The enterprise that I'm referring to is the company you now work for, and the future you need to envision is in terms of years not days or months. Visionary thinking comes in several different forms.

Being a visionary thinker means being strategic in your overall thinking process. Sure, you still need to maintain your foot on the gas in terms of day to day managerial details, but you also need to strategize the details of what your company can do in the future to maintain its competitive edge within its industry. Perhaps you've heard it said that the only constant in the world of business is change, because change is always occurring whether you know it or not. Competition in business can be fierce, and if you and your company owner or manager fail to take note of and heed the changes that are occurring, then your company may find itself eating dust instead of making dust. Strategizing the processes of how to stay competitive is a critically important part of being a visionary thinker and leader.

Take a moment to think about people who you might view as visionaries in their industry, and perhaps just in general. How about Richard Branson, or Steve Jobs, or Elon Musk, or Walt Disney? Or maybe you're thinking about Thomas Edison or Alexander Graham Bell, although each was an inventor, but aren't inventors the epitome of visionary thinking? I would say yes to that query, for inventors are in effect trying to see things not as they are but as what they could be. I for one am someone who would love to envision a world full of peace and mutual prosperity, but making that vision come to reality takes world leaders who share common values and common goals, which unfortunately is not the case today. Will that kind of world visionary ever be found?

When you think of a visionary do you think of any politicians as visionary thinkers? I see many of them as visionary speakers because that's what you hear during campaign stops, but I see very few of them as visionary realists. Medicare for All might sound like a wonderful idea to constituents and voters, but is it realistic in terms of cost and implementation? Your role as a new leader in your company is to think in terms of reality more so than conceptually. Your sense of what can actually be achieved is an important element of your strategic thinking because real results are what you will be judged on by your boss or owner. You will not be judged on what might have been, but rather only on what actually did occur.

Let's look at a minor example of strategic implementation versus visionary thinking. You have no doubt heard much talk around the country about raising the minimum wage to $15.00 per hour. Many companies, states and cities have already taken steps to begin actualizing the process of achieving that end result. You may or may not be a personal proponent of this wage increase. On one hand there is real justification for adopting the increase because far too many people are living on wages that are virtually impossible to live on. On the other hand there is real fear that the increases will have a different kind of cause and effect outcome, either by companies passing the wage increases on to consumers by raising prices, or by companies having negative earnings results. If you are the owner of the company neither of those outcomes is desirable on the surface.

The folks at McDonald's faced this issue head on by adopting a strategy that both reduced their dependence on labor and simultaneously achieved faster delivery times for their customer base. How did they do this? What McDonald's did was to implement the utilization of kiosks to change the food ordering process. This methodology would potentially reduce their overall labor hours and thereby help offset the hourly wage increases that would eventually become almost impossible to escape. Was this change strategic or visionary? Perhaps the only visionary part of the change was the realization that the wage increase would become a reality whether they liked it or not. But the main concept of the kiosks was far more strategic in effect because it was more reactionary than visionary. The wage increase to $15.00 per hour was not their idea, so the decisions they made were done so to respond to a need to maintain profitability objectives.

How do you become a visionary? I'm not sure I have the answer for you, but I would encourage you to read management books, leadership books, business news magazines and articles, and listen to whoever you deem as some of the great business leaders of our time. Being a great thinker is not necessarily something you're born with, so you will need to educate yourself to the best degree possible, and thereby develop yourself as someone who has the capability and capacity for looking into the future, much the same as looking into a crystal ball, as if such a thing actually existed.

FIGURE OUT WHAT'S IMPORTANT TO OTHERS

Okay, you've worked hard and you've been promoted. You have a job to do and you want to do the very best that you can. One of your key objectives is to make sure that you know what others expect of you and what is important to those around you. Your success to a large degree means that the people you work for need to be pleased with your performance. That also means that you need to know what their exact expectations are for sure, but you also need to find out what drives those expectation levels. What's important to your boss and/or to the owner? That's what you need to determine.

But when we talk about what's important, what do we mean by that? Well, one thing that might be important to your boss or owner is money. That means that they will look at your performance from a financial perspective. Your role, whatever it might be, most likely has some effect on the financial results of your company. You will need to keep a keen eye on everyone and everything in your arena that has an impact on margins and the delivery of positive financial results. That is what is important to the owner.

What else might be important to the owner and/or your boss? Well, maybe there are one or more people in your managerial realm that were hired by the owner or manager, or who are close friends or maybe even relatives of the owner or manager. Those people might be very important to the top leader, so you better find out who they are and what their exact relationship is to this manager. Should you not know that this has some importance to the owner or manager, you may end up on the wrong side of someone or worse yet you may very well fire someone you shouldn't. You may also find yourself saying the wrong things to the wrong people and then word gets back to the owner that you're don't know how to get along with others.

You will also need to find out what's important to those who work for you. Maybe some of them have family issues that affect their ability to work extended hours. Time for family issues will be important to those employees and you want to know this in advance. Maybe some of your employees don't think that advancement in the company is all that important. You will want to take this into consideration and perhaps temper your expectations from them. Maybe there will be some of your employees that have health issues and these issues have the potential for affecting their performance. You will want to know that these employees value their health and will expect you to know the importance to them, and to not take undue advantage of some personal imperfection.

Knowing yourself is one thing, but knowing others is an important aspect of managerial leadership and success. Make sure that you take the time to study other people and their habits, as well as talking to them in depth to better understand what is important to them in their job and in their personal life.

JAMES W. BENDER

PLANNING YOUR NEXT MOVE

I am sure that at this point you're wondering how and why you should be planning your next move when you just got the promotion you're been working towards. Hey, I just got this job, why would I want to think about the next one, you're asking? Yes, you just got your new promotion, you're right, but now is the ideal time to at least give some thought to your career path in general. If you worked hard to earn, and receive, your recent promotion, then you are undoubtedly the kind of person who has some ambition, and if you have ambition then you need to plan ahead. Success in one's career does not happen by accident.

If you are in the manufacturing industry, as an example, then you might want to be thinking about your next move in terms of advancing your career with your current company or maybe changing companies or maybe even changing industries. In fact you could have these same thoughts regardless of what industry you work in today. Many people in today's work environment believe that changing jobs is an occurrence that should happen almost as often as changing one's underwear. I'm not sure that is quite the route to take with your career, but I do believe that charting your course is an integral step in the process.

Let's use McDonald's again as an example of looking forward with regard to your career. In this example we will assume that you have worked for a locally owned and franchised McDonald's for over a year. You started out doing odd jobs like cleaning, trash removal, and some cooking. The owner of the enterprise likes the work that you've done and they offer you a promotion to full time cook, which comes with a nice pay raise. No one works for you with this new job, and you work for the assistant manager. You know that the owner of this restaurant also owns a number of others and you have heard that they are buying a few more. You realize that there is some upward movement possible with this company and you begin to think about strategizing a career path.

The first question you want to ask yourself is this one - what job would I ideally like to have and why? Is it the head cook or the assistant manager or the general manager or do you want to someday be an owner of your own McDonald's? Or, maybe you want to use the experience that you will gain at this restaurant as a springboard to land a position with a higher end restaurant instead of a fast food joint. These are all good things to think about as you start your new job as a full time cook. By thinking ahead you are enabling yourself to learn as much as you can about other aspects of the business while you are performing your current job as a cook. You are beginning to chart a course of action for your career path, and you are using every minute of every day as a sponge. You are soaking up any and all information possible and you are eager to talk shop with the owner whenever they are at your location.

Let's use another example. You have worked for a locally owned moving company for about a year as a moving helper. In this job you are basically carrying furniture in and out of homes to and from a moving truck. You have done a nice job and the owner has noticed that you are personable and reliable. The owner comes to you and asks you if you would like to be trained as a driver, starting out driving a straight truck, but perhaps later going on to driving a tractor trailer. The new job would be a promotion and have a nice pay raise to go with it. You would be the crew leader on every job when you are the driver. What should you be thinking about as you ponder this new opportunity?

Well, first, do you think you would enjoy driving and leading a crew of two or three other moving helpers? Second, do you think you would want to be a driver for a moving company long term? Is this a career that you would enjoy or is this just a job to pay bills? Once you become a driver I would speculate that your career path would continue down that path for quite some time. Are you prepared for that kind of lifestyle? If not, have you thought about anything else that you might want to be doing for a living? Could you talk to the owner about a different career path after your succeed at the driving role? Maybe you could be an operations manager or have some other managerial role in the company. Do you know enough about the company and the owner to know if you would enjoy working at this company longer term?

These are all good questions to be asking yourself as you ponder your very next step. Sure, a promotion is a great achievement for you, but you want to use this opportunity to begin a serious dialogue with yourself and with the owner of the company as a means to strategize a future course of action. Thinking carefully about your career choices is critical in order that you take charge of your own destiny. It's far better for you to be in control than to allow others to take control.

I have seen people make choices for all the wrong reasons and then later regret making those choices. As an example I have seen managers make the decision to take their best salesperson and promote them into a position of sale management. I have seen a great salesperson make the decision to take a sales management job to only later regret doing so after they fail miserably at their new role. I have seen someone who is a great auto mechanic take a role as the service manager, only to later regret taking a job that they were not very good at and not very happy doing.

Sometimes people accept a promotion because they think it's the right thing to do and it allows them to make more money. They accept the job without giving it much thought at all. They don't strategize the future impact of the new job and they don't try to forecast a career chart of sorts that can occur as a result of the promotion. Not every promotion is necessarily a good one just because it happens. Some of them are dead end promotions with very little upside. Some of them occur because someone wants you to fail and this is their way of showing you the door. Some are a result of someone just trying to take advantage of you. Some of them require a certain knowledge and skill set that you don't really have at this point in time. That would be a recipe for disaster.

The bottom line is this - study every opportunity carefully for your own benefit.

www.ingramcontent.com/pod-product-compliance
Lightning Source LLC
Chambersburg PA
CBHW031836170526
45157CB00001B/325